C L A S S I C
Table Linens

SYMBOL OF EXCELLENCE PUBLISHERS, INC.

Dedication

This book is lovingly dedicated to the
women in our lives — our mothers, mothers-in-law,
and grandmothers — who gave us a love for
beautiful needlework and instilled in
us an appreciation for
family tradition.

Phyllis Hoffman
Barbara Cockerham
Juanita Martinez
Janice Ritter

Library of Congress Catalog
Number: 84-052380
ISBN: 0-932437-00-1
Manufactured in the United States of
America

Classic Table Linens

Editors: Phyllis Hoffman
           Barbara Cockerham
           Juanita Martinez
           Janice Ritter

Contents

INTRODUCTION 6

PLACEMATS 8
Oriental Accent 10
Spring Oval .12
American Wildflowers 14
Royal Iris. 18
The Herb Collection 20

TABLECLOTHS 24
Southern Legacy. 26
Queen Anne's Lace 28
Simple Elegance 30
Wayside Wildflower Bouquet 34
Elizabeth's Herb Wreath 36
Blue Splendor 38
Autumn's Glory 40
Berries In Season 42
Shy Violets .44

TABLE RUNNERS 46
Simple Elegance 48
Vanessa's Rose 50
Traditional Markings 54
Pineapple Motif 56

ACCESSORY CLOTHS 58
Arlington Bridge Cloth 60
Vineyard Crumb Cloth 64
Plantation Pineapple Hutch Cloth 66
Nosegay Bread Cover. 68

CARE OF LINENS 71

PLAN A PROPER FIT FOR YOUR
TABLECLOTHS 72
Proper Cutting Techniques. 72
Proper Piecing Techniques 72
Proper Centering Technique 73
Stitching Suggestions 73

CHARTS. 74
American Wildflower 74
Elizabeth's Herb Wreath 76
Southern Legacy. 84
Queen Anne's Lace 87
Simple Elegance 92
Wayside Wildflower Bouquet 98
The Herb Collection 107
Lavendar. .107
Bee Balm .108
Comfrey 109
Borage 110
Chamomile 111
Tansy. 112
Santolina. .113
Pink Yarrow and Fern Leaf Yarrow . . .114
Traditional Markings 115
Shy Violets 118

CREDITS 120

SHOPPERS GUIDE 122

Introduction

A new definition of elegance in dining is evolving as families recognize that mealtimes are social highlights in their lives. The ambience created in the dining area is as important as the food which is served.

With a new awareness of the value of these times shared comes the opportunity to express yourself creatively and establish traditions with cross stitched table linens.

CLASSIC TABLE LINENS was designed and published through our desire to provide you with the challenge of stitching for your home in a new way. The table linens which are pictured in this book will certainly be passed as heirlooms to future generations. Ranging from very intricate designs which require many pleasant hours of stitching to simple designs used on specialty fabrics, we have included something for the stitcher at every skill level.

Your home is a reflection of you. Express yourself individually. If your lifestyle calls for frequent use of a formal dining room, invest time in creating a cross stitched masterpiece as a focal point for your formal dinner parties. Nine tablecloth charts are included in this book and five are major pieces bearing intricate designs.

In most homes, table linens used for family meals are seen much more often than those reserved for holidays and parties. Since your family is more important than any guests, strive to make those everyday meal settings as special as the attractive ones you use when hosting parties.

If placemats play an important role in your meal service, you will delight in the collection of designs presented for that use. Placemats require little fabric and finishing is easy. The designs we have chosen are lovely and can dress up your table with a minimum of effort on your part. Choose your favorite fabric, and finish the piece in a manner suitable to the fabric and the design.

Table runners and accessory cloths are important pieces and help complete your table linen collection. Two of the table runners included carry intricate designs and two were chosen for their quick-to-stitch quality. All four can be used to enhance your dining room decor. Accessory cloths have a variety of uses, require little fabric, and make wonderful gifts.

Set the mood for your meals or for a room by your choice of table and accessory linens. Pretty tables continue in importance whether the occasion calls for elegant formal dining or a simple casual dinner. Every meal offers an opportunity for fresh creativity using table linens.

Stitch your own linens for the satisfaction and pride of doing it yourself, and for the challenge of customizing a piece especially for your home. Allow your fine handcrafted table linens to help you turn every meal into a celebration and make every dinner hour a time to linger.

Relaxing together over a candlelight dinner for two, sharing a stimulating account of the day's activities with the children around the dining table, or hosting a garden party for 20, make every mealtime special.

CLASSIC TABLE LINENS is for you, to help you start now to establish a tradition with your handwork. Stitch your pieces with pleasure and use them with great pride.

Placemats

ORIENTAL ACCENT

THE HERB COLLECTION

AMERICAN WILDFLOWERS

ROYAL IRIS

SPRING OVAL

When work, school, and club activities keep your family on the go, treasure the mealtimes you do share. Start by creating a pleasant, relaxed atmosphere, complete with an attractive table.

Whether your meal is served in a kitchen breakfast nook or in a corner of a great room, placemats are an excellent choice for your table. With a wardrobe of placemats for your dining areas, you can make each meal a visually pleasing time.

Because placemats are small, stitching a set does not require a large investment of time or money. These versatile cloths are easy to stitch and laundering care is simple.

A variety of designs is presented in this chapter for your consideration. From Oriental to country wildflowers, you can choose a design to suit your decorating taste.

Designs from two full-size tablecloths have been adapted and scaled to work well on placemats. Matching napkins bearing the motif will add a crowning touch to your table setting.

Six designs from the Wayside Wildflower Bouquet are used on a specialty fabric to give an informal look to the lovely flowers. Stitch all six, or select your favorite and repeat it on a set of four or six mats.

Designs from Elizabeth's Herb Wreath are used on two sets of placemats. Worked on light brown linen, the look compliments the country kitchen. A second set of herbs stitched on Lugana gives a formal look to use with your finest china, silver and crystal.

Consider adding variety to your placemat collection by choosing interesting new fabrics and colors which contrast or blend with your dining areas.

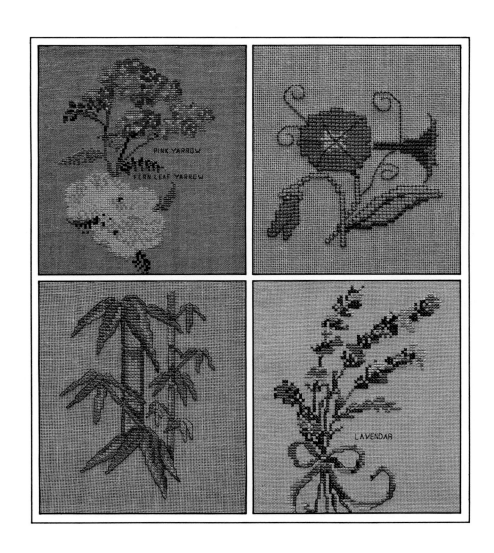

ORIENTAL ACCENT

he simplistic lines and natural colors of bamboo make Oriental Accent a pleasing addition to your placemat collection. A touch of the Orient can be used in decorating any dining room, from the most modern chrome and glass to the stately traditions of mahogany and Queen Anne.

The Oriental Accent tea cloth featured is slightly larger than a standard placemat. It is used as a companion for the custom designed Japanese tea service. Treasures of this kind call for cloths which are specially colored and stitched to highlight the intricacy of the Oriental design.

A single cloth bearing the Oriental Accent design would make a wonderful display cloth for Oriental treasures.

Worked over two threads on 25-count Driftwood (#23) Dublin linen from Joan Toggitt, Ltd., the placemat shown is self-fringed.

BAMBOO

	DMC	
X	470	olive green - dk.
0	471	olive green - med.
•	472	olive green - lt.
	469	outline for entire bamboo
●	597	aqua - dk.

1. Cut fabric 19″ x 14″.
2. Stay stitch ½″ from edge on all four sides. Fringe.
3. Place design 1½″ from left side and 2″ from top.

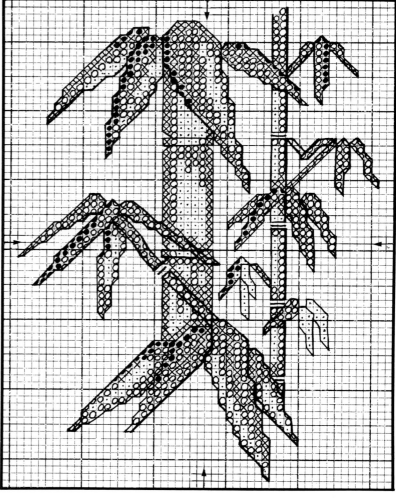

SPRING OVAL

S oft spring pinks and greens are used to stitch the blossoms and stems of the free-form Spring Oval. Featured in a casual setting, the tray cloth accents the soft muted colors of the china.

The treat of having breakfast in bed can be enhanced with the beautiful cross stitched tray cover. The colors of the blossoms could be altered to compliment the china which will be used on the breakfast tray.

Use the design as it appears on the tray cloth, or stitch it as a horizontal design to accommodate the shape and size of the china you plan to use on the cloth.

An excellent choice for placemats or crumb cloths as well as tray cloths, Spring Oval is shown stitched on Sand (#332) Dublin linen from Joan Toggitt, Ltd. The model is stitched over two threads on the 25-count linen and is finished with a narrow hem.

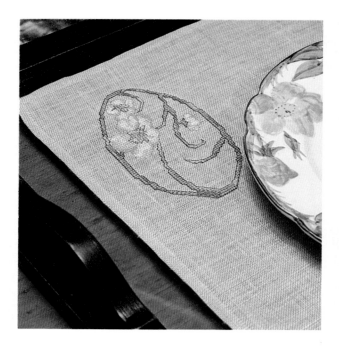

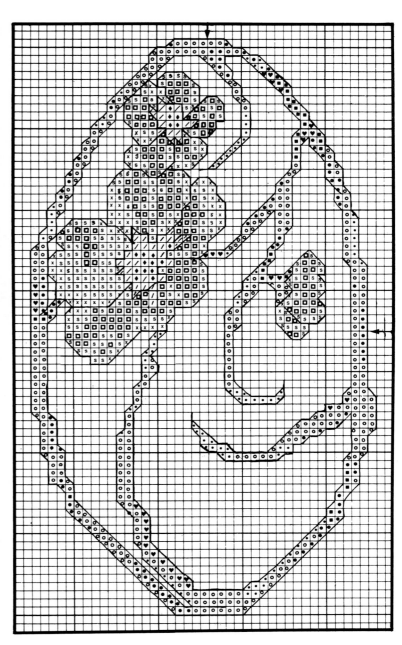

OVAL FLOWER DESIGN

	DMC	
▫	818	lt. pink
s	776	med. pink
x	3326	dk. pink
——	899	outline for flower petals
/	973	yellow
♦	783	topaz
	780	outline for flower center
•	472	lt. olive
o	471	med. olive
●	470	dk. olive
——	469	outline for oval vines
♥	598	lt. aqua
■	597	dk. aqua

AMERICAN WILDFLOWERS

Bring wildflowers to your table with a striking combination of Alice cloth and single American Wildflower blossoms. Six wildflowers from the Wayside Wildflower Bouquet tablecloth have been hand-picked and charted for placemat use.

The vivid blues of Morning Glories and the brilliant yellows of the Ox-Eye Daisy have been selected to enhance placemats of taupe and white Alice cloth used on a table set for mid-morning breakfast. A stroll around the yard fills the vase with wildflowers for the perfect centerpiece.

Similar to a five-inch plaid, 27-count Alice cloth is 100% cotton and is highlighted by a heavy white interwoven thread. The designs are stitched over two threads, filling the square with color. The placemats are self-fringed. Alice is a product of Joan Toggitt, Ltd.

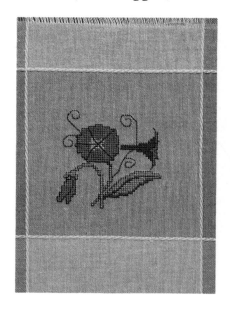

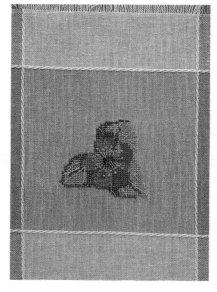

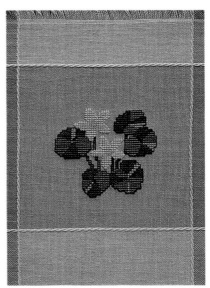

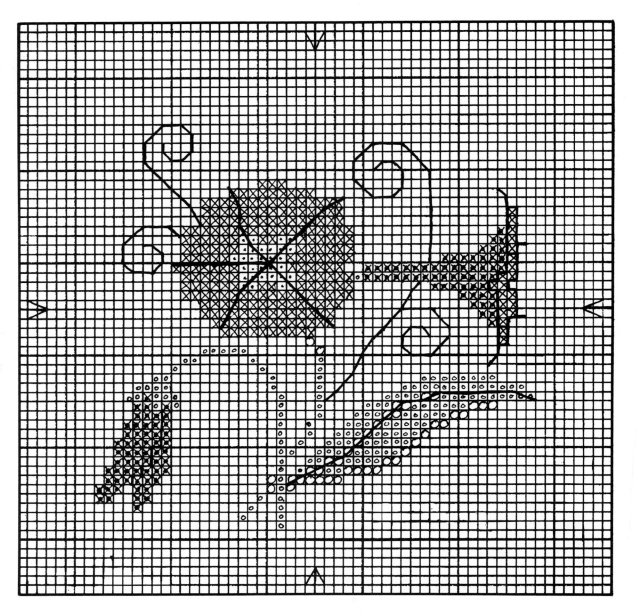

MORNING GLORY

	DMC
X	794
●	Blanc Neige
●	472
X	798
O	581

Outline petals and petal vines in 798. Do not outline between blue and white in center of flower.
Outline leaves, stems and tendrils in 581.

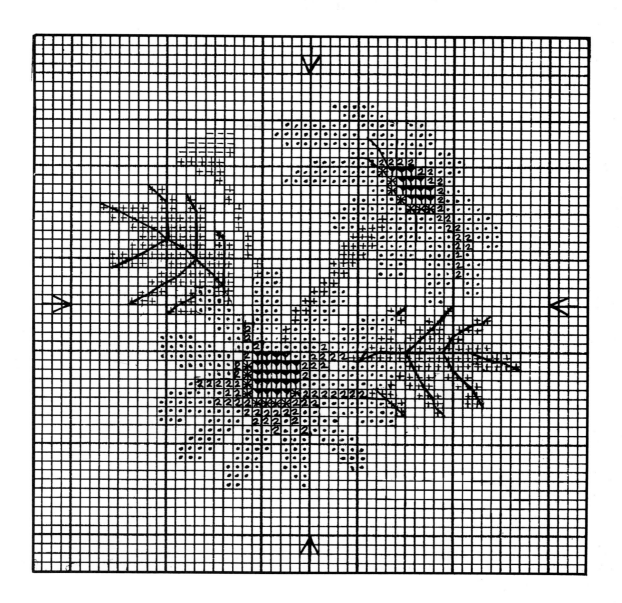

OX-EYE-DAISY

	DMC
—	3364
+	3363
•	Blanc Neige
2	Ecru
✳	434
Y	725

Outline petals in 535. Outline centers in 434. Outline stems, leaves and veins in 3362.

Charts continued on page 74

ROYAL IRIS

Sharp, vivid design and bold color selection make Royal Iris an attention getter! The stylized Oriental-look design is shown worked on a hunt board cloth of blue Alice cloth.

Alice cloth is woven with a heavy white thread which defines the five-inch squares on which the Royal Iris design is placed. The design is stitched over two threads on the 27-count 100% cotton fabric from Joan Toggitt, Ltd. The hunt board cloth is finished by self-fringing.

Shown in a traditional setting, the cloth tastefully harmonizes with the tray (Circa

1780) and surrounding wall accessories. The strength of the design also makes Royal Iris an excellent choice for placemats to be used with a contemporary glass-top table.

Royal Iris can mingle with any decor and hold its own for any size cloth you select.

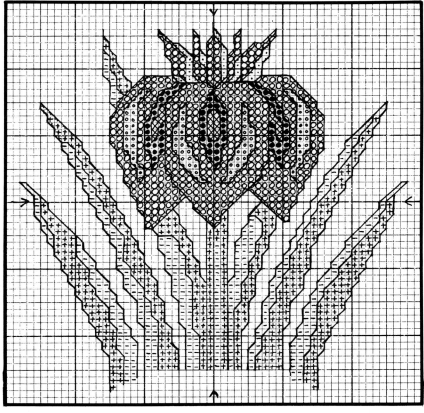

1. Cut fabric to desired length.
2. Stay-stitch ½" from edge on all four sides. Fringe.
3. Stitch design in desired square.

	DMC	
o	3689	lt. mauve
O	3688	med. mauve
——	3687	outline for flower petals
−	907	lt. green
+	906	med. green
——	905	outline for leaves
●	793	lt. blue
x	794	med. blue
——	792	outline for blue center of flower petals
•	743	yellow

THE HERB COLLECTION

raditional herb designs with intricate shading and detail are charted for individual use on placemats. The same herbs are entwined in Elizabeth's Herb Wreath, a tablecloth design featured in this book. For stitchers who prefer placemats on their tables, The Herb Collection provides a compatible design which can be used on formal or informal cloths.

The group of yellow herbs is shown stitched on 26-count light brown linen from Wichelt Imports, Inc. The placemats provide a soft compliment for the collection of teapots serving as the centerpiece. The beautiful cloths remain on the table between meals to lighten the dining area.

Mauve herbs are shown stitched on 25-count Bone Lugana. The beautiful mauve tones blend with the fabric background and lace trim to produce an elegant formal

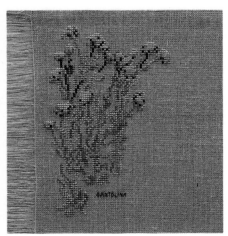

BORAGE

BALSAM

COMFREY

look. Shown in a traditional dining room with accompanying china, crystal and silver, these herbs move into the spotlight at the grandest dinner party. Both the fabric and the Nutria Beige Christina lace are from Joan Toggitt, Ltd.

Centerpiece for the formal herb placemats is arranged with coordinating flowers which accent the placemats without overpowering the stitched design. Soft muted green napkins play on the colors in the green foliage of the herbs.

The Herb Collection placemats are designed for a narrow table. Careful attention should be given to the shape of your table when sizing placemats. Standard placemat sizes should be altered to fit your special needs and to achieve the look you want for your table.

The color and texture of fabric selected for placemat background will determine the look resulting when the stitched piece is completed. Choose a finishing method or edging in keeping with the style set by the fabric you use.

The entire Herb Collection taken as a whole or in part lends itself to casual or formal dining. The choice is yours.

Charts begin on page 107

Tablecloths

SOUTHERN LEGACY   BLUE SPLENDOR

WAYSIDE WILDFLOWER BOUQUET

SIMPLE ELEGANCE   BERRIES IN SEASON

ELIZABETH'S HERB WREATH

AUTUMN'S GLORY   SHY VIOLETS

QUEEN ANNE'S LACE

*H*and stitched full-size tablecloths are truly heirloom pieces. Made of the finest quality fabric and floss, these linens will endure indefinitely.

Whether you prefer to entertain buffet-style or at seated dinners, formal dining calls for full-size tablecloths. Set the mood for your formal dinner with a cross stitched tablecloth chosen to enhance your dining area.

This chapter features nine tablecloths selected for the variety of cross stitch designs and finished looks which they present. Designs range from traditional motifs and stylized flowers to elegant herbs and wildflowers. Choosing your design from this wide range enables you to stitch your favorite in colors which work well in your room. Keep in mind the room's paint colors, wallpaper design, draperies and accessory pieces when planning your tablecloth.

Instructions for making the designs work on your table are also included. Make sure the fabric is properly sized to fit the table before stitching the design.

The manner in which the cloth is finished will be a key factor in the overall look of the piece. Choose lace insertion and edging with the same care given to selecting the fabric for the tablecloth. The weight and feel of the trim should be compatible with the fabric you are using.

When your cloth is complete, use it with pride and pleasure. Heavy linen cloths should be used over a silence-pad which fits the table. Lighter weight linens and those made with lace insertions can be used directly over the table to allow the beauty of the wood to show through. In a like manner, an undercloth in a color which plays on the colors of the stitched design can be used.

Included in this chapter with formal linens of classic styles are smaller informal cloths to use as table toppers or kerchiefs.

SOUTHERN LEGACY

Beautiful magnolia blossoms reminiscent of moonlit Southern nights are teamed with other flowers to produce an elegant cloth suitable for all dining occasions. The creamy petals and waxen leaves of the magnolia make it a favorite far beyond the bounds of the Deep South.

Featured in a formal dining room, the green hues of the tablecloth are complimented by the antique English ironstone tea set. Adaptable to fit any size table, the Southern Legacy cloth will be the center of attention at your formal gatherings.

The model pictured is stitched over two threads on 25-count Green (#776) Dublin linen and is finished with Buttercream Marie Antoinette Lace. Both linen and trim are from Joan Toggitt, Ltd.

Charts begin on page 84

27

QUEEN ANNE'S LACE

Queen Anne's Lace, that airy blossom appearing along country roadsides between May and September, is charted for your dining table in a splendid intricate design. Closer examination of this wildflower, also known as Wild Carrot, reveals an intriguing geometric pattern.

To accurately re-create the airy look, stems of the Queen Anne's Lace are stitched first, then the white blossoms are stitched over the stems to create a dimensional effect. Accompanying these pale flowers, the plant leaves are stitched separately to complete the center trellis design.

Scallops of blossoms edge the table top in a repeating pattern. Diagrams indicate how this repetition is easily adapted to any table shape or size. A common connecting stitch allows any section of the graph to join another.

The Queen Anne's Lace tablecloth is shown dramatized with green plants and prepared for a snack luncheon buffet. A more formal occasion could be highlighted with a bouquet of Queen Anne's Lace as a centerpiece. The cloth is a showpiece and can be used for all occasions.

Fabric selected for the cloth is 25-count Driftwood (#23) Dublin linen with Ice Green Isabella lace trim. Both fabric and trim are from Joan Toggitt, Ltd.

Stitching over two threads produces dramatic white blossoms. The light floss colors of Queen Anne's Lace make it an ideal design for use on medium to dark colored fabrics.

Charts begin on page 87

29

SIMPLE ELEGANCE

*T*raditional borders and flowers grace any table and blend with any decor.

Impressive end designs are linked by a connecting ribbon band which is centered on each side with a flower cluster of large and small blossoms. For variety, the ribbon bands can be omitted and replaced with additional side motifs. Longer tables may require the use of two or three side design sections repeated. For round tables, only the end designs are stitched.

For an antique look, use subtle colors. Dramatize more modern decor with the use of vivid colors suggested. Use your imagination as you adapt this elegant design for use in your home.

Simple Elegance is shown stitched over two threads on 32-count Cream (#52) Belfast linen. The tablecloth is finished with Devonshire Cream Julianna lace insertion and edged with matching Christina lace. Fabric and trim are from Joan Toggitt, Ltd.

Color suggestions on next page

31

Simple Elegance Tablecloth

Corals

Mauves

Blues & Lavenders

Taupes

Pinks

Yellows   *Charts begin on page 92*

33

WAYSIDE WILDFLOWER BOUQUET

More than 25 delicate wild-flowers from all regions of the country are gathered into this garland of color. Nature paints the flowers with vivid colors which have been interpreted in embroidery floss for your dining table.

Stitched over two threads on 22-count China Rose (#414) Oslo, the Wayside Wildflower Bouquet is used as a contrasting highlight in the apothecary blue dining room. Coloration of the floral design provides several shades of green, blue, yellow and mauve that will play off any room color.

The centerpiece and auxiliary flower

arrangement are limited to white flowers featured in the cloth. This plays up the wildflower theme but does not compete with the tablecloth for attention.

Finishing is as important as stitching. The beauty of the stitching must be enhanced by the trim selected. Victoria Lace in Devonshire Cream is used to edge the cloth. With its teardrop shape, the exquisite lace adds the perfect finishing touch to the work of art. Fabric and lace are from Joan Toggitt, Ltd.

An alternate color scheme is given to allow you to change the cloth color to a neutral such as off-white, cream, or pale grey. American Wildflower placemats using six of these designs are featured in this book.

Chart on page 98

ELIZABETH'S HERB WREATH

*T*his lovely design from nature brings to mind a colonial herb garden basking in the sun on a summer day. Herb gardens have been of vital importance throughout history. They were meticulously planned to provide a year's supply of seasonings for food and ingredients for medicinal purposes.

In colonial times, herbs became important to artists who recorded botanical history through painting. The beauty of ordinary plants surfaced as details were painted. Subtle hues and complex shading were noted as bright colors faded into soft tones. Herbs are now of great importance to stitchers who paint with floss on fabric.

Use Elizabeth's Herb Wreath cloth for candlelight dinners on the terrace, afternoon tea with a friend, or to grace a special table at a wedding reception.

The cloth shown is stitched over two threads on 32-count cream (#52) Belfast linen from Joan Toggitt, Ltd. The cloth is edged with Buttercream Marie Antoinette lace, from Joan Toggitt, Ltd.

The Herb Collection, featured in this book, is a single presentation of each herb for placemat use.

Chart on page 76

BLUE SPLENDOR

egal crescents of stylized flow-ers nestle in the corners of the woven pattern of Patrice Cloth, a product of Craft World.

The open center of the Blue Splendor design allows the use of a pretty center-piece on your dining table. Flower colors in the design can be changed to suit your preference.

A geometric design stitched along the sides between the heavy woven lines com-pletes the Blue Splendor look.

Stitch count: 70w x 66h

☐ 322   Navy blue - vy. lt.
Outlined in 311 - navy blue-med.

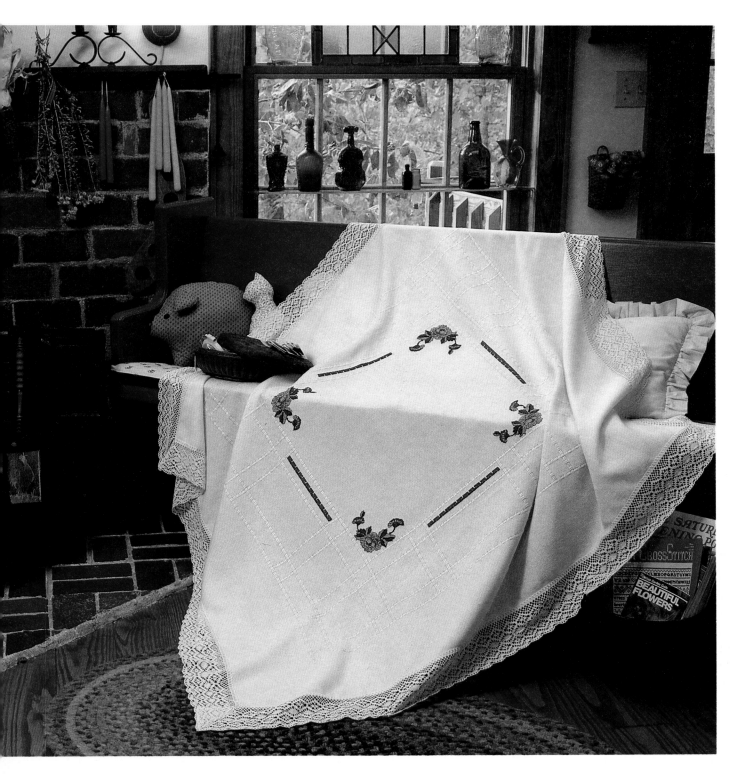

Patrice cloth is designed with a heavy woven thread which forms a banded border in the center of the 52-inch square pattern repeat. Corner squares are 60 x 60 threads, while longer side bands are 120 x 60 threads. The fabric is 14-count.

	DMC	
□	322	Navy blue - vy. lt.
•	3325	Baby blue
◆	890	Pistachio green - ultra dk.
#	367	Pistachio green - dk.
/	368	Pistachio green - lt.

Outline flowers and inside of flowers in 311. Outline leaves & underside of small flowers in 890.
Position flowers in corners of material.

AUTUMN'S GLORY

*I*nterior design in recent years has made popular the table kerchief or overlay cloth. The prefinished overlay cloth pictured has been whisked away to the crisp outdoors for an early autumn picnic.

Whether inside or outside, the versatile size of the overlay cloth makes it a perfect choice for serving snacks, hosting picnics, or gracing a small round table.

Autumn's rich hues are caught in the colorful leaves stitched on the 5½ inch, 18-count corner inserts of the ecru polished cotton cloth from Tish and Amy Originals. The cloth is finished with cluny lace.

Pretty calico napkins in rust and browns

will complete the table setting if this design is used for a dining cloth. Centerpieces of autumn flowers, fruits or vegetables will make your table an attention getter. Perfect for giving and keeping, this cloth is easy to stitch.

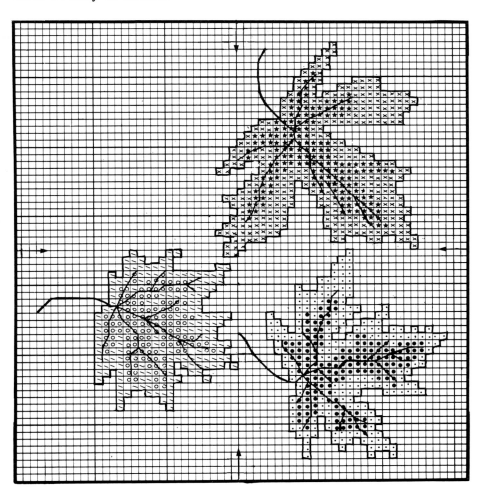

	DMC	
•	676	Old gold - lt.
●	680	Old gold - dk.
/	725	Topaz
o	921	Copper
x	922	Copper - lt.
★	355	Terra cotta - dk.

Outline all leaves, stems and backstitching in 801 - coffee brown-dk.

Stitch count: 60w x 57h

BERRIES IN SEASON

*L*uscious red strawberries trail between the borders formed by interwoven red threads on 22-count Kitchen Hardanger. Surrounded by family pieces, antique purchases, and flea market finds, the Berries In Season cloth completes the warm inviting look of this country kitchen.

The gingham undercloth is tucked under at the hemline to produce a balloon appearance which incorporates modern decorating touches with old fashioned cross stitch design.

Stitched over two threads, this cloth is easy to complete and is breathtaking in a country kitchen as well as in a more modern kitchen decor. The square top cloth of Kitchen Hardanger, a Wichelt Imports fabric, is finished with white fringe.

	DMC	
x	666	Christmas red - brt.
-	3345	hunter green - dk.
•	744	yellow
+	3346	hunter green
c	3348	yellow green - lt.

Stitch count 85 x 24

SHY VIOLETS

*Y*ou can enjoy lovely violets year round, regardless of the season, with table linens bearing the Shy Violet design. The popularity of violets is revived with this design trio cross stitched on white linen.

Shown in a cool white-on-white setting, the neutral tones are interrupted with the contrasting table underskirt, allowing the purple of the undercloth to peek through the lace insertion. Lace edging accentuates the beauty of the violets.

The Shy Violets cloth is shown stitched on 32-count White (#51) Belfast linen over two threads. Juliana insertion lace is used to join the squares and the cloth is edged with Isabella lace. Linen napkins are made of the same fabric and trimmed with narrow Christina lace which matches lace used on tablecloth. The elegant Pearl White laces are a perfect trio for use with the violet designs. Fabric and lace are from Joan Toggitt, Ltd.

Charts begin on page 118

Table Runners

PINEAPPLE MOTIF

TRADITIONAL MARKINGS

SIMPLE ELEGANCE

VANESSA'S ROSE

By varying the fabric type and color, and by choosing a variety of designs to stitch, you can complete a table runner for every season and every mood. From plain to fancy, these oblong pieces of fabric can hold an important place in your table linen collection.

Table runners are gaining in popularity as homemakers recognize the runner's value in presenting a "finished" table look. Cross stitched runners can be used to add a touch of elegance and color to your meals. Adding a simple centerpiece and matching or plain placemats and napkins will afford a table worthy of your best china and your specialty menus.

For variety, use a cross stitched table runner as a between meal highlight for your dining table. Select floss colors which compliment the decorator colors in your room.

Table runners can be used to top solid color full-size tablecloths for an interesting look. Select a simple motif from the runner and stitch matching napkins for use with this layered effect.

The series of alphabets in this chapter can be used in many ways. Shown on a personalized table runner, the letters are ideal for monogramming placemats, napkins and plain tablecloths.

Simple Elegance Placemats

SIMPLE ELEGANCE

Change your decorating pace by using an elegant cross stitched table runner to replace the centerpiece as the focal point of your dining room. The fresh decorative look of a runner is sure to be the center of attention.

Classic styling and subtle colors allow Simple Elegance to blend with any decor. Seven color options are shown with the Simple Elegance Tablecloth.

Colors selected for the runner can be accessorized with undercloths and napkins used on your formal dining table. Top your favorite "stand by" solid cloth with a Simple Elegance Runner in your favorite colors.

Soft tones of Dusty Miller plant surrounding the hurricane globe reflect the colonial colors chosen for the Queen Anne decor shown. Stitched in antique colors over two threads on 26-count Ivory Sal-Em fabric from Carolina Cross Stitch, the runner is finished with purchased tatting.

Charts begin on page 92

49

VANESSA'S ROSE

*E*ntwining rose blossoms and buds offer a fresh look at an old favorite set on a formal table runner. The rose, an American flower often synonymous with love, adds elegance to any setting, and what better place for a cross stitched rose than in the center of a runner or full-sized tablecloth.

The chart given is half of the design, to be completed by turning the chart and stitching to complete the motif.

The table runner pictured is stitched on 25-count Wedgewood Blue Lugana and features soft melon shades in the blossoms. The runner is finished with Christina lace in Devonshire Cream.

CENTER

Shaded area indicates a portion of the chart from the previous page. Use as a guide in aligning stitches only.

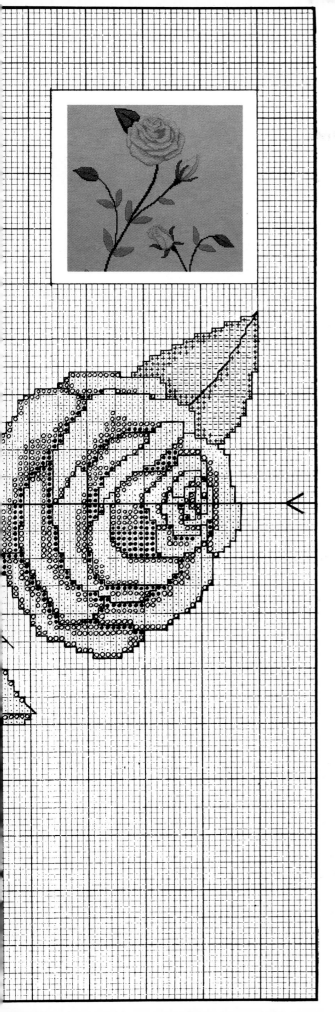

VANESSA'S ROSE

Legend	DMC On Light Blue	DMC On White	
.	948	225	
o	353	224	
●	352	223	
—	522	3052	
+	520	3051	(also leaf outline)
/	524	3053	
——	350	221	(rose outline)

General Instructions:
Supplies needed for runner as shown:
 Fabric - Wedgewood Blue Lugana
   25 stitches to the inch
   51" x 16" piece
 Lace - 4 yards of Christina lace in ivory.
 Floss - DMC colors indicated for blue
   fabric
 Stitching - Runner design is stitched over
 2 threads on this fabric

1. Cut the fabric to the appropriate
   length. Note - if a different thread
   count is used the length and width of
   fabric must be adjusted accordingly.
2. Fold fabric to find the center.
3. The arrow on the graph indicates the
   center of the design.
4. Stitch one side entirely then turn the
   chart and stitch the other side being
   careful to keep center stitches aligned.
5. Narrowly hem fabric edges.
6. Wash and block fabric.
7. Pre-shrink lace before attaching.
8. Attach lace by hand or machine. The
   corners of the lace shown are mitered.

TRADITIONAL MARKINGS

*P*ersonalized table linens have been popular for centuries. The age-old custom of marking linens still enjoys a degree of popularity today.

Modern day monograms call for the first initital of the last name to be used as a large center initial. When using three initial's, the husband's first initial is used as a small intial to the left of the center, with the wife's first initial balancing the monogram as a small initial on the right of center.

The table runner shown is a prefinished runner band cut the desired length and hemmed.

Chart on page 115

PINEAPPLE MOTIF

Yellow and white Arno, a vividly patterned Aida fabric, makes a perfect background for the pineapple motif used in this table runner. The motif would be equally at home on napkins, placemats and accessory items such as tumblers and mugs which use fabric inserts.

Colored vertical and horizontal threads create the four-inch squares on the 12-count 100% cotton fabric from Joan Toggitt, Ltd. The design is stitched over one thread on the runner pictured.

The 42-inch runner is used favorably on an antique sideboard to pull together the green and yellow color scheme of the room. The two-fold purpose of decorating and protecting furniture is achieved with this simple runner.

The play on color can be achieved with bright evenweave fabrics and simple adornments. Arno is available in blue, pink, green, and brown, and with simple color changes, the pineapple design can be adapted to any color cloth.

The runner, edged with purchased trim, is equally lovely with self-fringed edges.

DMC

- 469 avocado green
- o 726 topaz - lt.

Outlining & backstitching in 469.

Outside rows of pineapples are stitched in every other square beginning in square to right & left of center with the tops of pineapples toward the center of the material. Center row of pineapples has design in every other square with one pineapple facing in one direction and next pineapple facing in opposite direction.

Stitch count: 38 x 15

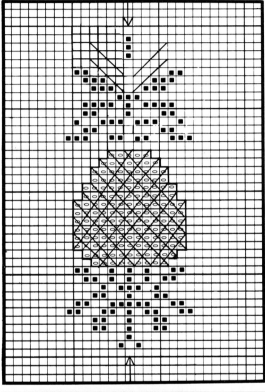

Accessory Cloths

ARLINGTON BRIDGE CLOTH

PLANTATION PINEAPPLE HUTCH CLOTH

VINEYARD CRUMB CLOTH

NOSEGAY BREAD COVER

*W*hen you need an important gift for a new bride, give a gift of yourself and your time by starting or adding to her table linens. From bread basket covers to hutch cloths, accessory table linens make wonderful gifts to stitch for special relatives or friends.

One linen piece which can be used at almost every meal is the bread basket cover. Easy to stitch and bind, the piece can go casual for family meals by using Aida or Hardanger stitched over two. Dress up the accessory cloth for use with a silver tray by choosing linen or lugana and adding lace or tatting at the edges.

Crumb cloths, smaller than placemats and designed for use when dessert or fruit and cheese is served, make nice additions to any linen closet. Shown worked on Hopscotch™, the design is framed by the bold color woven into the fabric. The design would be equally appealing worked on white or off-white Aida or bleached linen.

The Arlington Bridge Cloth included in this chapter makes a colorful addition to any card game. Sized to fit a card table, the cloth works well as an overlay cloth for a refreshment table. Floss colors in the design can be changed to suit your decor.

Some accessory cloths have a two-fold purpose - to protect the furniture on which they are used and to add a decorative touch to the room. By using a hunt board cloth or hutch cloth, you can utilize antique pieces for serving without fear of damaging the finish. Cloths can be used to call attention to the furniture or a special accessory such as the antique punch bowl placed atop the Plantation Pineapple Hutch Cloth.

Let your accessory cloth collection grow as your time permits and as specific needs arise.

ARLINGTON BRIDGE CLOTH

*T*he tabletop corner baskets sport flowers mixed with the traditional diamond, heart, spade and club in an arrangement sure to draw favorable comments from any bridge fan. Baskets are used in two diagonal corners with sprays of flowers complimenting the remaining corners.

A companion design for score pads is shown stitched on a perforated paper score pad from Your Accents. The cover is reusable and comes with replacement pads making the stitched cover a permanent addition to your game. The cross stitch design also fits the tally from Your Accents. A set of tallies and score pads makes a wonderful gift for bridge playing friends.

When hosting several tables of bridge, you might choose to use the cross stitched Arlington Bridge Cloth on your refreshment table, and accent individual card tables with stitched tallies and score pads.

Stitched on 20-count Jobelan from Wichelt Imports, Inc., the cloth is finished with a three-inch self-fringe.

Breaks indicated by the curved lines on the graph show where the border pattern can be lengthened to custom fit the cloth to your table.

ARLINGTON BRIDGE CLOTH

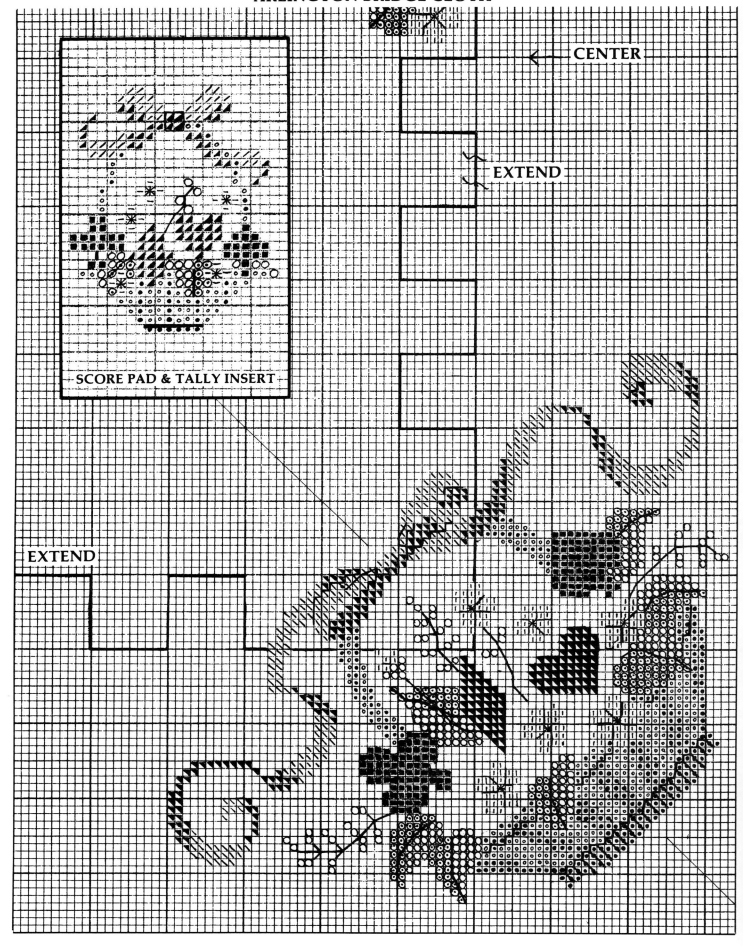

CENTER

EXTEND

SCORE PAD & TALLY INSERT

EXTEND

ARLINGTON BRIDGE CLOTH

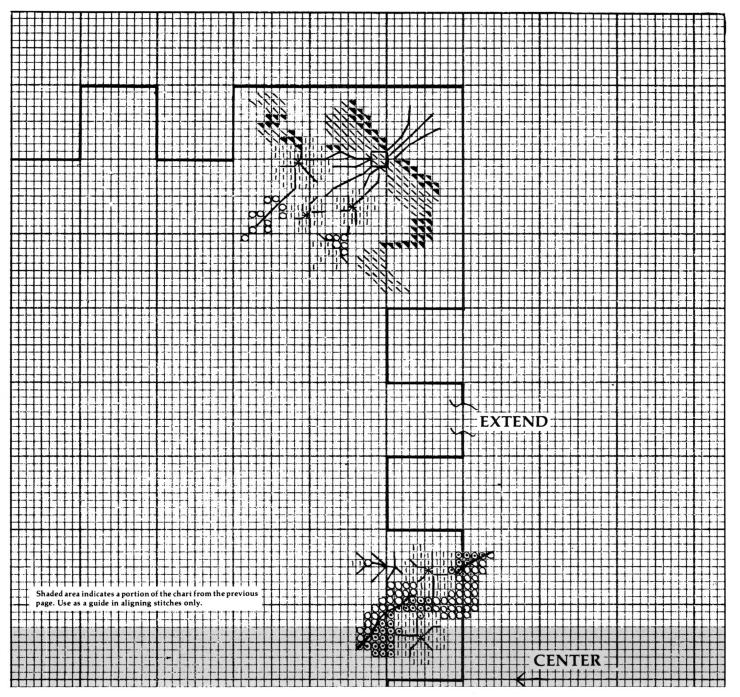

Shaded area indicates a portion of the chart from the previous page. Use as a guide in aligning stitches only.

EXTEND

CENTER

DMC
3371
335
326
3325
727
3348
3346
422
420
869 Basket outline
3345 Leaf & stem outline

Fabric - 53" square of Jobelan
20 count stitched over 2
1. Cut fabric on straight grain so the edge of fringe will be even.
2. Stay stitch 3" from edge on all four sides.
3. Fringe the edges.
4. Center the design on the fabric.

Prefinished score pad has perforated paper insert for stitching complimentary design. This small design will fit tallies made by the same company.

VINEYARD CRUMB CLOTH

S un ripened rich-colored clusters of grapes have for years seemed symbolic of a leisurely life in which dessert parties and afternoon tea hold a special place. These special times call for special table linens.

Let cross stitched crumb cloths bearing the Vineyard design be a part of your tradition as you establish the wonderful practice of tea with a friend, or revive the custom of hosting dessert parties.

Dusty Rose Hopscotch™ from Charles Craft, Inc. was selected for these square

crumb cloths using the Vineyard pattern stitched on the 14-count center square. The fabric was cut 14½"-inch squares and self-fringed to finish.

Table decorations in the same color family strengthen the mauve design. Foods served can compliment the cloths perfectly and make an attractive centerpiece.

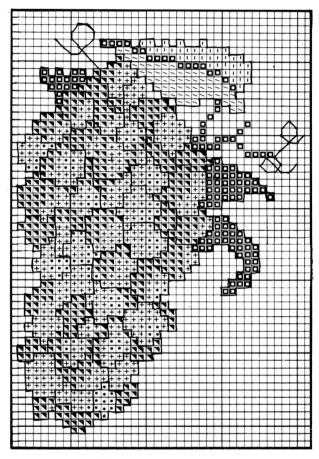

	DMC	
◻	500	Blue green - vy. dk.
\	502	Blue green
ı	504	Blue green - lt.
◥	316	Antique mauve - med.
+	778	Antique mauve - lt.
•	224	Shell pink - lt.

Outline leaves in 520 - Fern green-dk. Backstitch stems in 520.
Outline grapes in 315 - Antique mauve-dk.
Stitch count: 56w x 38h

General Instructions:
1. Cut fabric into 14½" squares so the cream check is the center.
2. Stay stitch ½" from edge on all four sides. Fringe.
3. Center design and stitch.

PLANTATION PINEAPPLE HUTCH CLOTH

Since the early days of this country, the pineapple has been displayed as a symbol of welcome and hospitality. An easy way to bring warmth and a feeling of welcome to your kitchen is through the use of the Plantation Pineapple design.

The hutch cloth shown is a beautiful accent piece to be used on side pieces of furniture in your kitchen or dining area. It serves as a protective cloth for the antique hutch and calls attention to the antique punch bowl.

The Plantation Pineapple hutch cloth is stitched over two threads on 26-count light brown linen from Wichelt Imports. The piece is finished with a 1½-inch blind hem on the back and sides, while the front is fringed and knotted.

If you choose to fringe your hutch cloth, allow eight inches of fringed material so that the knots can be tied with ease. Clip the tassels to the desired length.

DMC		Backstitch
□	368	
x	320	
✱	367	....
	890	+++
o	3013	
△	3047	
•	3046	
■	3045	
	869	∿∿
	898	————

1. Cut fabric 27½" long x 16" wide.
2. Pineapple starts 6¼" from lower cut edge. Center design.
3. Cloth is hemmed on 3 sides with 1½" hem.
4. Fringe 2½" on lower edge. If knots are desired, every 10 threads are tied.

NOSEGAY BREAD COVER

*H*ot bread and pastries are nestled securely in the Nosegay Bread Cover. The nostalgic floral design adds a touch of elegance to the easy-to-stitch cloth.

The simple flowers and old fashioned doily are reminiscent of time spent learning to bake rolls, biscuits and breads — a time of fun and pleasure.

Nosegay Bread Cover is stitched on 14-count Pewter Aida and is bound with grey bias tape. This versatile design lends itself to your personal interpretation through your choice of background color and binding choice.

For a more formal look, stitch the design on linen and add lace or tatted trim. Finished in this manner, the basic cross stitched piece is suitable for lining silver or pewter bread trays.

Stitch this lovely cloth for a new bride and coordinate colors to compliment her china pattern, or make one for a young lady you are teaching to cook. The cloth will have special meaning for you both.

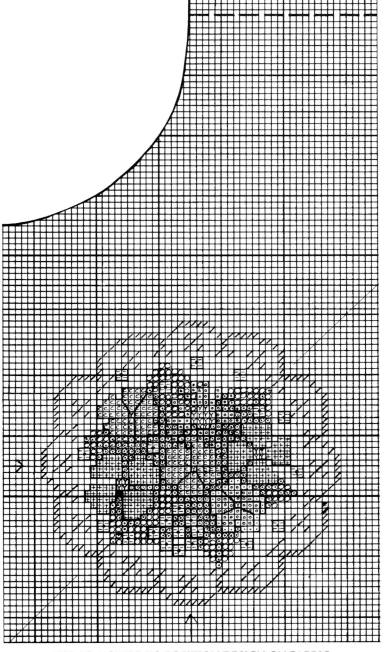

USE AS A GUIDE TO POSITION DESIGN ON FABRIC.

PATTERN REPRESENTS ¼ OF BREAD COVER.

The pattern for the bread cover and the chart are on the following page.

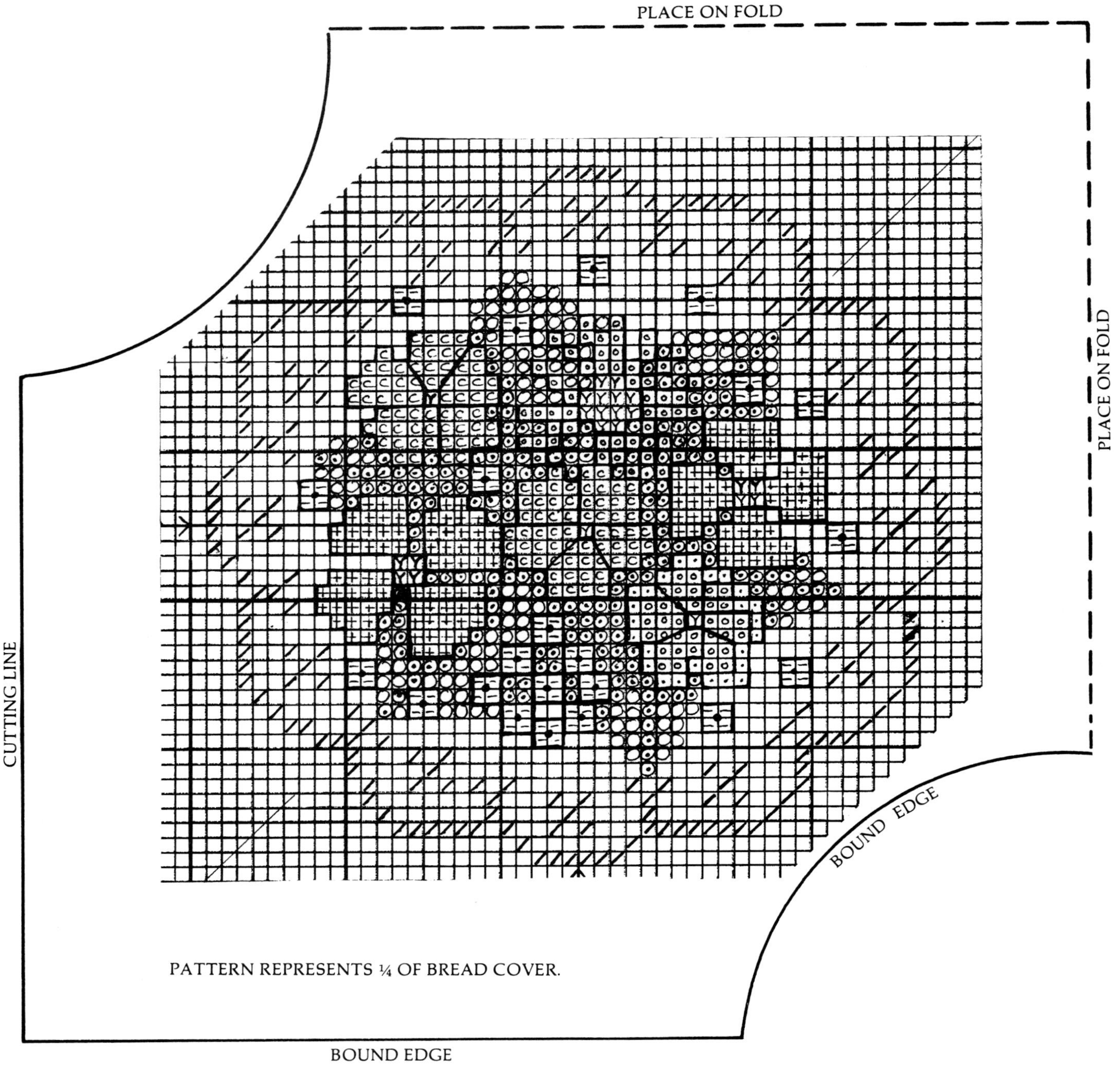

PATTERN REPRESENTS ¼ OF BREAD COVER.

PLACE ON FOLD

PLACE ON FOLD

CUTTING LINE

BOUND EDGE

BOUND EDGE

NOSEGAY BREAD COVER

DMC #		Outline	
O	504	————	844
⊙	502		
/	414		
—	800		
+	799		
c	760		
Y	3078		
·	778		
o	3041		

INSTRUCTIONS:

1. Pattern and graph are for 14-count fabric - approximately 16" square.
2. Place pattern of correct scale on fold at dotted line.
3. Turn under edges and attach lace or tatting.
4. Work design on one corner only.

CARE OF LINENS

Fine linens deserve the best possible care. Proper care also enhances the look of your table linens and assures their long life.

The most desirable way to store linens is flat, un-ironed and unfolded. Press just before using. While a china cabinet or hutch drawer will provide adequate space for storing place mats, and perhaps small accessory linens, full sized cloths such as those required by a truly formal dinner will require another method of storage.

For larger linen cloths, a method of rolling for storage is recommended. A cardboard tube, a minimum of one inch in diameter, should be covered with a clean white fabric or acid-free tissue paper. The cloths can then be rolled gently around the tube and covered with more white fabric or acid-free tissue.

If it is not possible to roll larger pieces of table linens, these may be gently folded and stored where no other item is placed atop the linen. Never press in creases or folds. Linen thread is very durable, but it also tends to be brittle so creases and folds increase the possibility of thread breaking or cracking.

Caution should be exercised in selecting a location for storing linens. Avoid exposure to excessive heat or dampness. Do not place linens in plastic or airtight bags. Linen is a natural fiber and should be allowed to breathe.

Table linens made of cotton or synthetic fabrics can be washed, dried and pressed with the same care afforded today's fine fabrics. Items made of linen fabric should be gently washed by hand in mild soapy water and rinsed thoroughly.

Remove as much water as possible by gently pressing the cloth between large thick terry towels. Drape over two or three clothes lines. Do not pin. Pinning the cloth to the line will result in a distortion of the thread lines. If a clothes line is not available, cover a shower curtain rod with thick towels and drape the cloth over it.

Do not use bleach on linen pieces. Use other standard stain-removing practices.

When linens are thoroughly dry, store un-ironed. Press just before using. Steam pressing adds moisture to the fibers, and if linens are stored after such pressing, mildew could result.

PLAN A PROPER FIT FOR YOUR TABLECLOTHS

The charts given here show standard tablecloth sizes for rectangular, oval and round tables. If you are fortunate enough to own an antique dining table, check carefully to determine the proper size needed for your special cross stitched cloths. Most tables built in more recent years will be covered by the following charts.

To determine the size your cloth should be, measure the width and length of your table. Add 20 inches to both dimensions to allow for a 10-inch drop on all sides. Consider the number of people to be seated at the table. If you add a leaf or leaves to your table, be sure your guiding measurements reflect those additions. A proper fitting cross stitched cloth will be a gift of yourself for today and for the future.

STANDARD TABLECLOTH SIZES

52x70 Rectangle	52x70 Oval	60-inch Round
60x84 Rectangle	60x84 Oval	68-inch Round
60x92 Rectangle	60x92 Oval	70-inch Round
60x104 Rectangle	60x104 Oval	

PROPER CUTTING TECHNIQUES

There is a right way to cut evenweave fabrics. To insure proper length and width, the fabric must be cut on the grain.

As shown in the photographs, linen is cut by pulling a thread, then cutting in the "track" left by the removed thread.

The other evenweave fabrics (Aida, Hardanger, etc.) have a grain that is easy to see for cutting guides.

Whatever fabric selected, the straight edge is important for fringing, hemming, or attaching trim.

PROPER PIECING TECHNIQUES

Many of the evenweave fabrics used for tablecloths are not wide enough to cover the table top plus the proper 10" overhang on all sides. The linen fabric used in this book is 55" wide.

Fabric is added to the sides as illustrated.

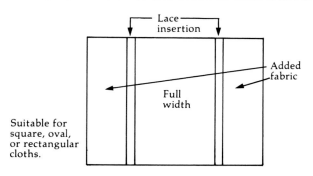

An example of this technique is used on the Simple Elegance Tablecloth.

Round cloths require piecing also. The additional fabric is added before the fabric is cut into the round shape.

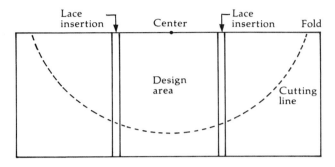

NEVER PIECE FABRIC IN THE AREA WHERE THE DESIGN IS TO BE STITCHED.

PROPER CENTERING TECHNIQUE

The placement of the design on a large piece of fabric can be tricky. These simple steps make centering easy.

Fold the fabric lengthwise to find the center. As shown, place a long center running stitch the entire length of the cloth.

Fold the fabric to find the center of the width. Place a long running stitch on the center line.

The two basting threads will cross in the center of the cloth. This will provide five reference points for stitching.

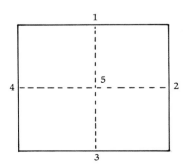

Leave basting threads in until stitching is finished.

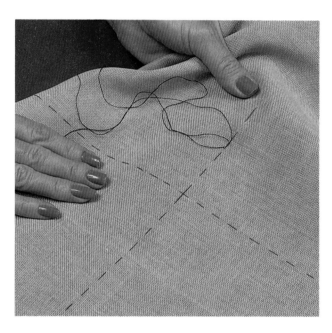

STITCHING SUGGESTIONS

Before stitching the design, "bleed" the floss individually by washing it. Simply remove the bands, wash in mild soapy water, rinse thoroughly, then blot. Lay floss aside to dry, being careful to keep the floss from tangling.

After cross stitched design is finished, wash and block the cloth before attaching the lace or trim.

Pre-shrink all insertion lace and edging lace before attaching it to the fabric.

AMERICAN WILDFLOWERS

COMMON PERIWINKLE

	DMC
◢	333
•	Blanc Neige
■	3362
+	3363

Outline petals in 333. Do not outline betwee purple and white of flower centers. Ove, stitch centers in 333. Outline stems and leave in 580, leaf veins in 472. Work medium Fren knots in 3046.

Outline in 3371.

CROSS-VINE

	DMC
2	Ecru
r	3350
■	3362

Outline in 3371.

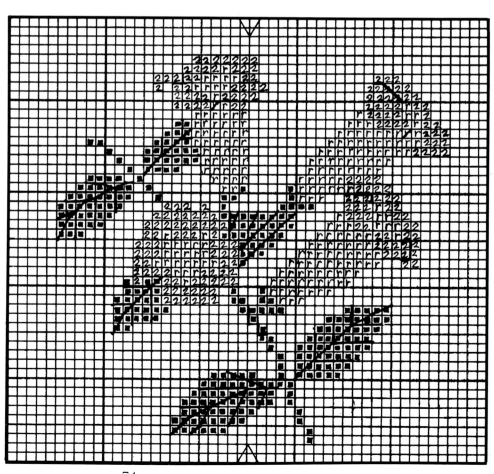

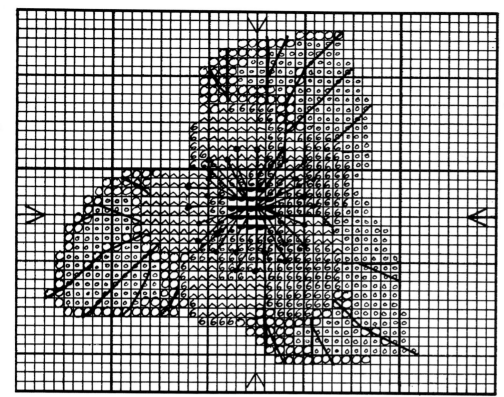

WILD ROSE

	DMC
O	581
•	472
6	956
∧	957
⏾	646

Work medium French knots in 725, connect to center of rose with single strand 744 running stitch. Outline flowers in 3371, leaf veins in 502.

MARSH MARIGOLD

	DMC
O	744
⊙	725
•	472
⍦	580
Y	581

Outline petals in 725. Outline leaves and stems in 3362. Work medium French knots in 3046.

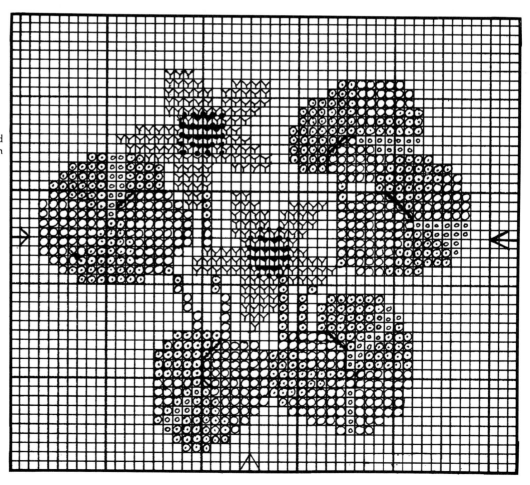

ELIZABETH'S HERB WREATH

Note the similarity between the following symbols: △ △ ▲ ◣ ⇕↑

	DMC	
△	221	Shell pink - dk.
▪	223	Shell pink - med.
•	224	Shell pink - lt.
=	225	Shell pink - vy. lt.
o	778	Antique mauve - lt.
c	316	Antique mauve - med.
●	315	Antique mauve - dk.
✶	319	Pistachio green - vy. dk.
н	320	Pistachio green - med.
п	327	Antique violet - dk.
↑	367	Pistachio green - dk.
ᴧ	368	Pistachio green - lt.
s	347	Salmon - dk.
℺	444	Lemon - dk.
L	524	Fern green - vy. lt.
/	522	Fern green
◆	520	Fern green - dk.
☆	550	Violet - vy. dk.
м	611	Drab brown - dk.
8	640	Beige grey - vy. dk.
J	642	Beige grey - dk.
З	644	Beige grey - med.
⇂	680	Old gold - dk.
∓	761	Salmon - lt.
φ	760	Salmon
v	725	Topaz
т	726	Topaz - lt.
⤳	727	Topaz - vy. lt.
◗	782	Topaz - med.
▼	783	Christmas gold
Y	822	Beige grey - lt.
◣	890	Pistachio green - ultra dk.
ℓ	369	Pistachio green - vy. lt.
#	935	Avocado green - dk.
←	834	Olive green - vy. lt.
+	902	Garnet - vy. dk.
§	3041	Antique violet - med.
0	3042	Antique violet - lt.
♥	3051	Green grey - dk.
ω	3328	Salmon - med.
△	3053	Green grey
∠		Snow white
◊	899	Rose red
▣	732	Olive green
ı	814	Garnet - dk.
z	778 & 225	Use one strand each.
⋇	3051 & 368	Use one strand each.

76

ELIZABETH'S HERB WREATH

Diagram indicates the entire chart and how it has been divided.

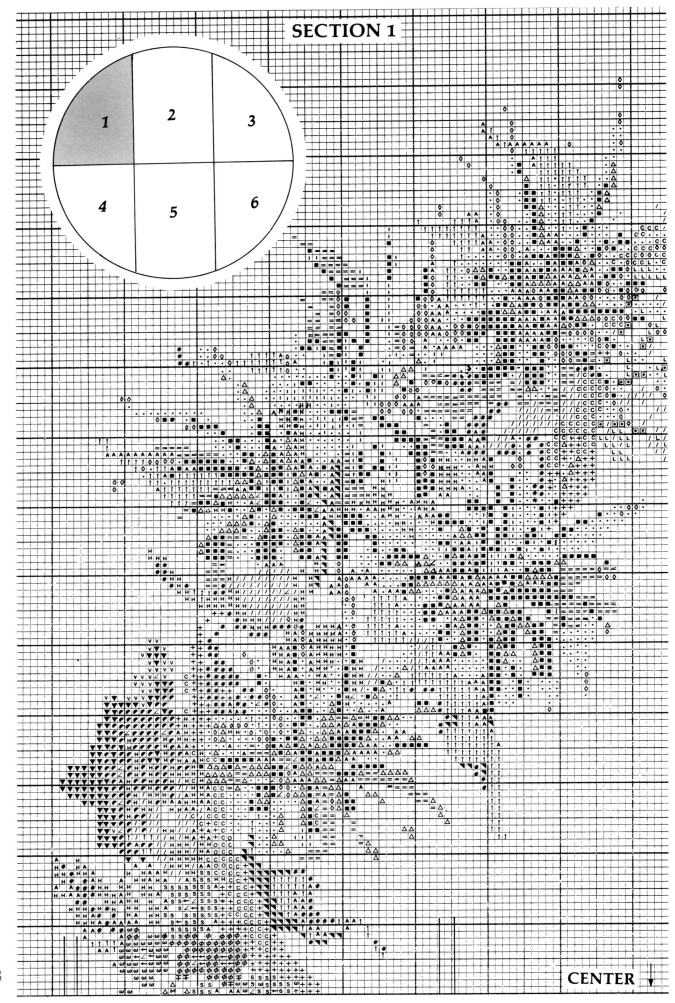

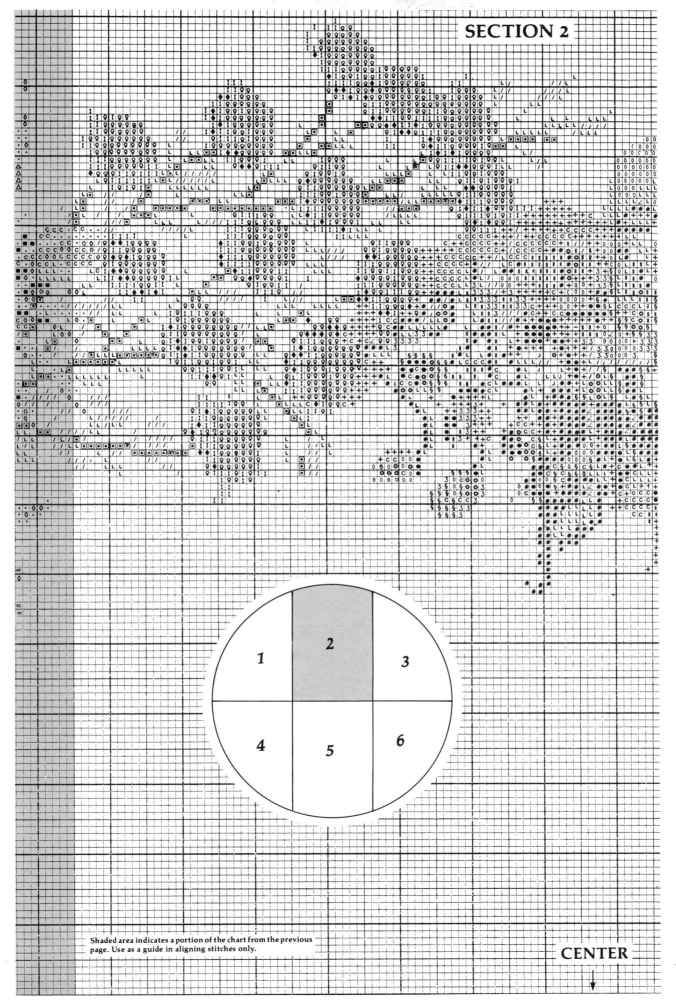

Shaded area indicates a portion of the chart from the previous page. Use as a guide in aligning stitches only.

CENTER

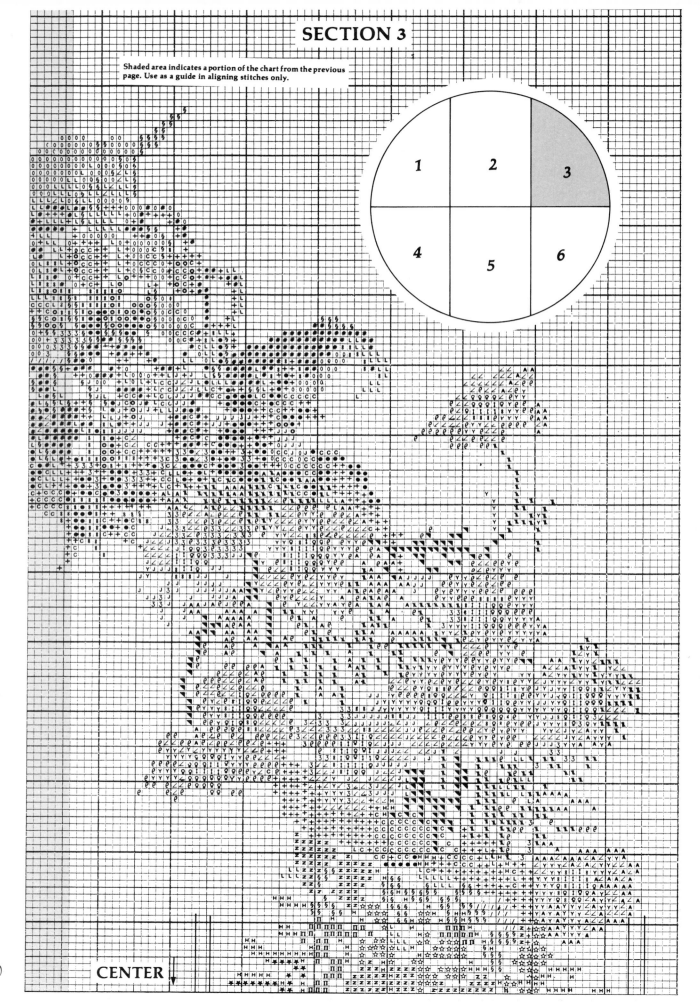

Shaded area indicates a portion of the chart from the previous page. Use as a guide in aligning stitches only.

CENTER

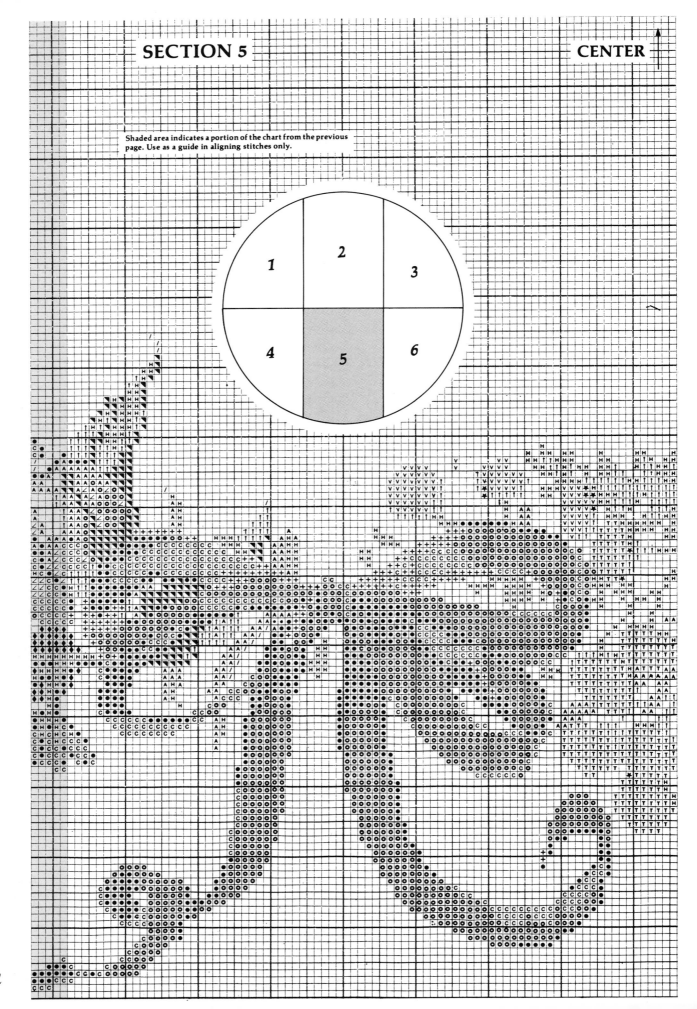

Shaded area indicates a portion of the chart from the previous page. Use as a guide in aligning stitches only.

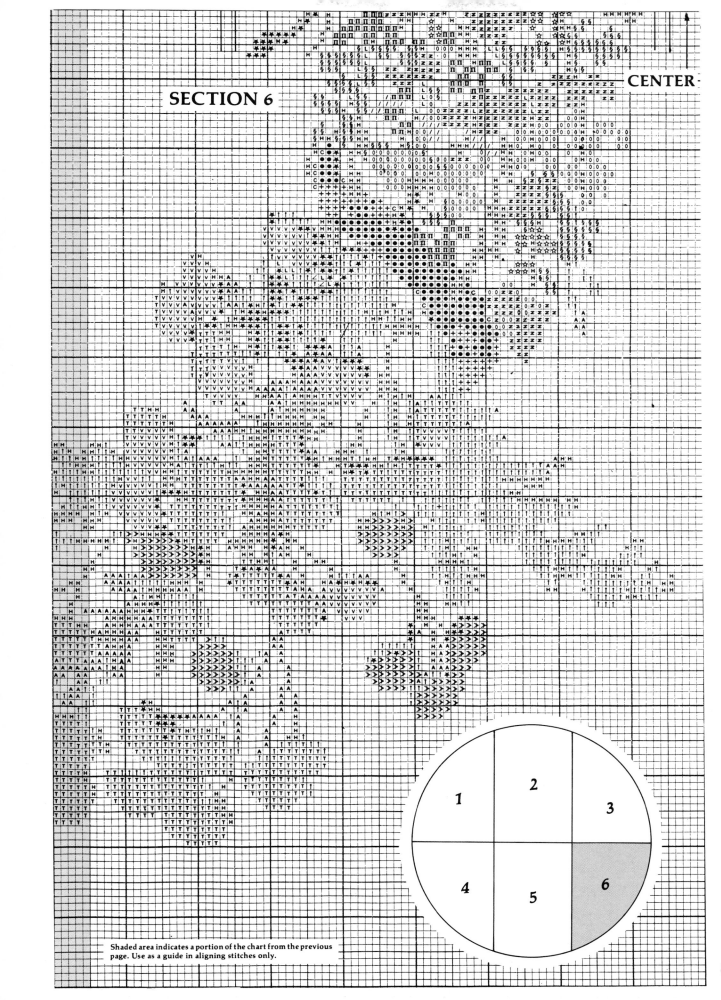

SECTION 6

CENTER

Shaded area indicates a portion of the chart from the previous page. Use as a guide in aligning stitches only.

CORNER SECTION

Join ✦ to ✦.

DMC
o	White
/	746
●	3047
·.	744
✕	334
☐	320
■	367
✱	781
Ø	760
⊙	3328
⋈	743

Backstitch white flowers in #645.
Backstitch yellow flowers in #781.
Backstitch pink flowers in #347.
Backstitch blue flowers in #311.
Backstitch all greens in #890.

Join ● to ●

USE AS A GUIDE TO POSITION DESIGN ON FABRIC.

Join ▼ to ▼ ◀

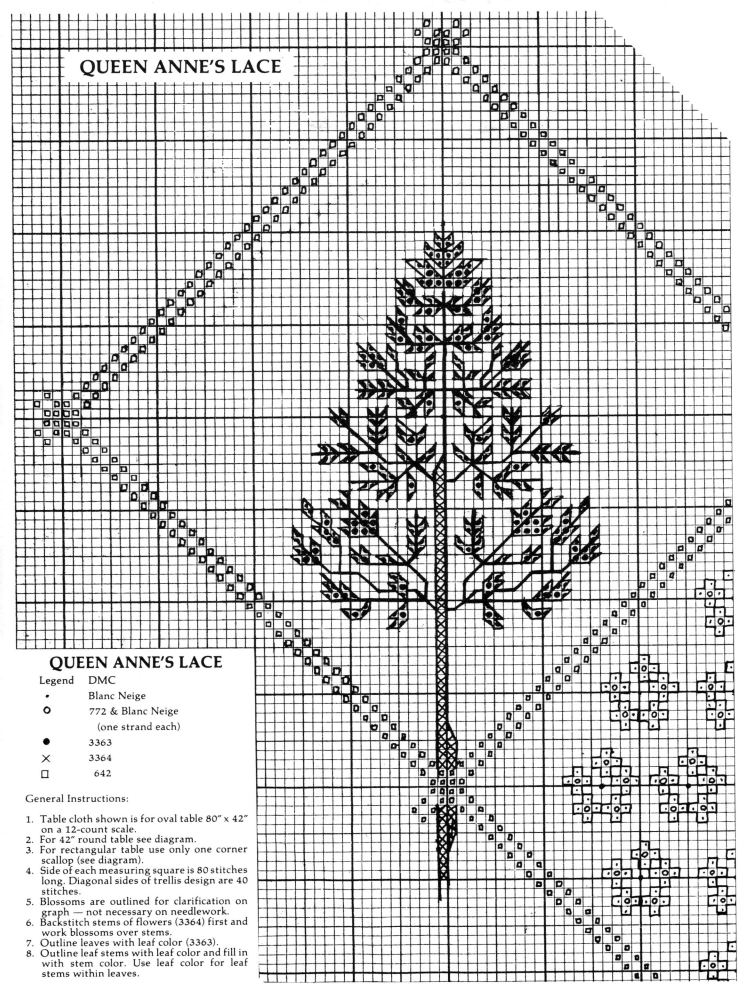

QUEEN ANNE'S LACE

QUEEN ANNE'S LACE

Legend	DMC
•	Blanc Neige
o	772 & Blanc Neige
	(one strand each)
●	3363
×	3364
□	642

General Instructions:

1. Table cloth shown is for oval table 80" x 42" on a 12-count scale.
2. For 42" round table see diagram.
3. For rectangular table use only one corner scallop (see diagram).
4. Side of each measuring square is 80 stitches long. Diagonal sides of trellis design are 40 stitches.
5. Blossoms are outlined for clarification on graph — not necessary on needlework.
6. Backstitch stems of flowers (3364) first and work blossoms over stems.
7. Outline leaves with leaf color (3363).
8. Outline leaf stems with leaf color and fill in with stem color. Use leaf color for leaf stems within leaves.

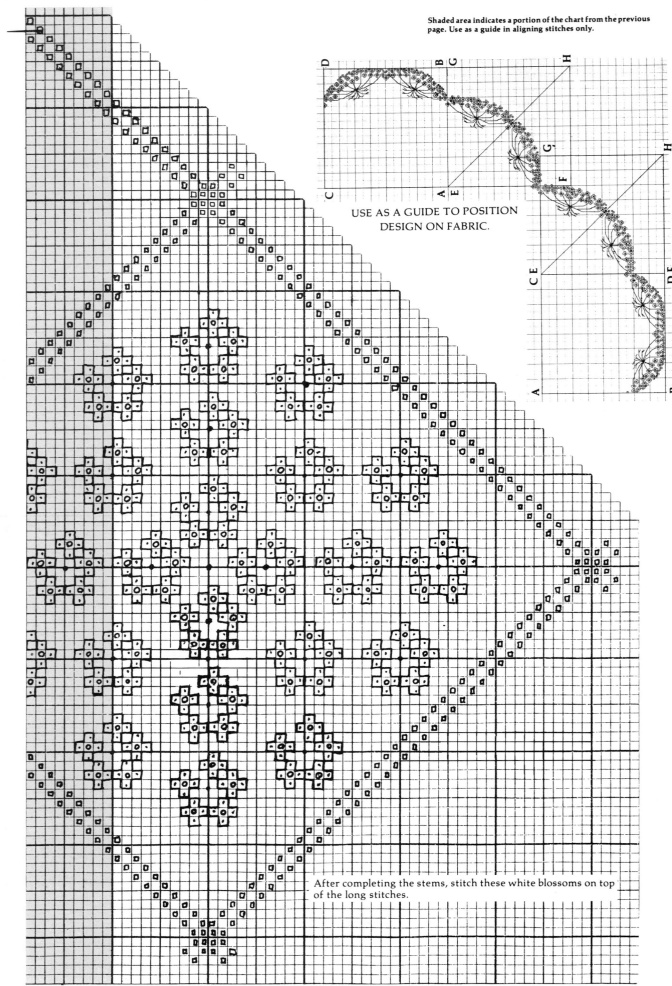

USE AS A GUIDE TO POSITION DESIGN ON FABRIC.

After completing the stems, stitch these white blossoms on top of the long stitches.

Before stitching white blossoms, stitch the stems first as noted on this chart.

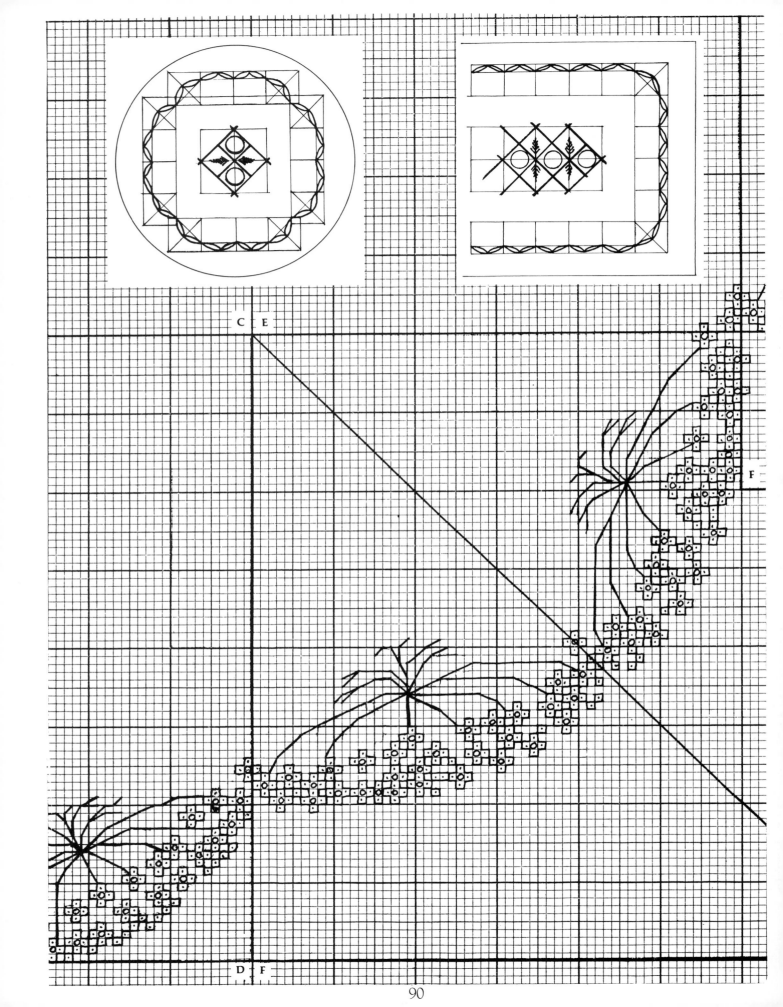

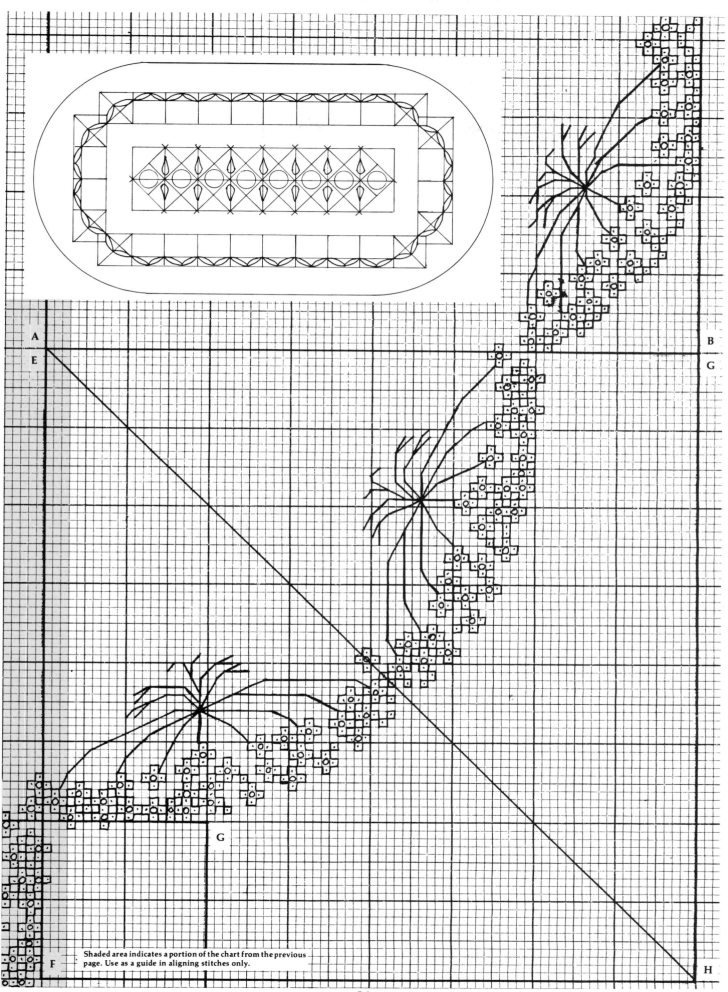

Shaded area indicates a portion of the chart from the previous page. Use as a guide in aligning stitches only.

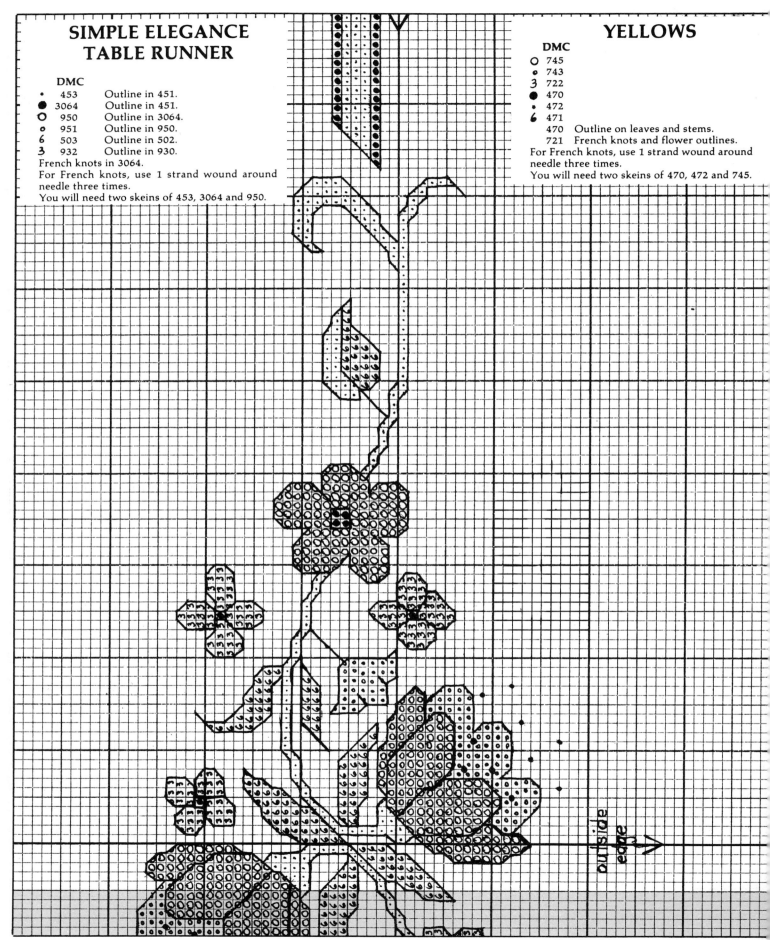

SIMPLE ELEGANCE
TABLE RUNNER

DMC

- • 453   Outline in 451.
- ● 3064   Outline in 451.
- O 950   Outline in 3064.
- o 951   Outline in 950.
- 6 503   Outline in 502.
- 3 932   Outline in 930.

French knots in 3064.
For French knots, use 1 strand wound around needle three times.
You will need two skeins of 453, 3064 and 950.

YELLOWS

DMC

- O 745
- o 743
- 3 722
- ● 470
- • 472
- 6 471
-    470   Outline on leaves and stems.
-    721   French knots and flower outlines.

For French knots, use 1 strand wound around needle three times.
You will need two skeins of 470, 472 and 745.

outside edge →

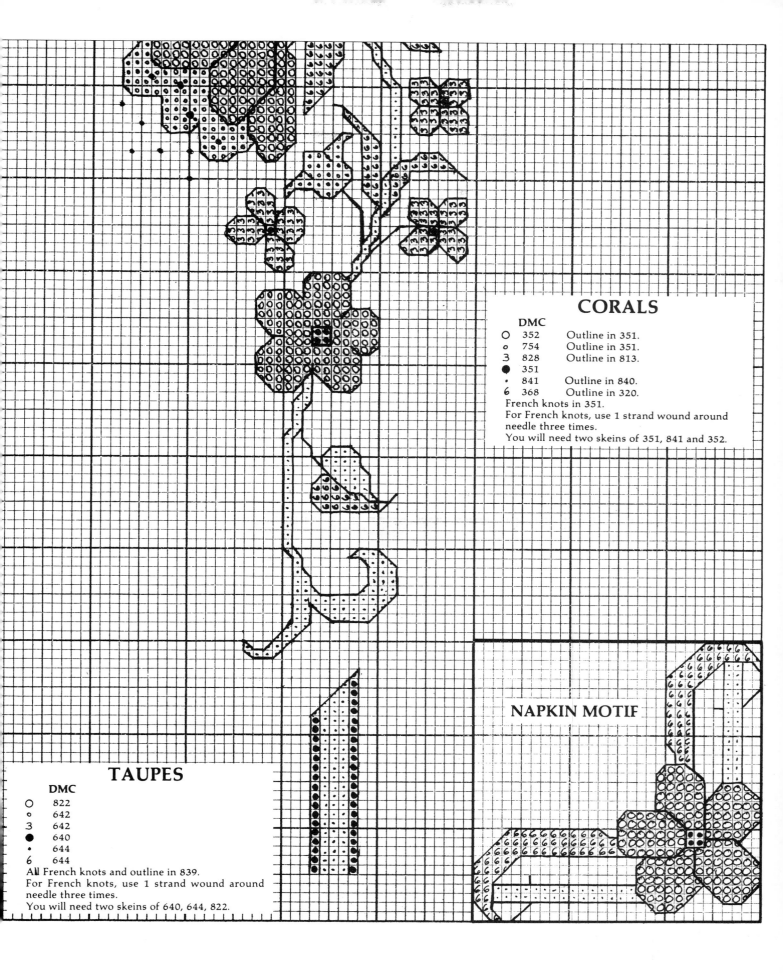

CORALS

	DMC	
O	352	Outline in 351.
o	754	Outline in 351.
3	828	Outline in 813.
●	351	
·	841	Outline in 840.
6	368	Outline in 320.

French knots in 351.
For French knots, use 1 strand wound around
needle three times.
You will need two skeins of 351, 841 and 352.

NAPKIN MOTIF

TAUPES

	DMC	
O	822	
o	642	
3	642	
●	640	
·	644	
6	644	

All French knots and outline in 839.
For French knots, use 1 strand wound around
needle three times.
You will need two skeins of 640, 644, 822.

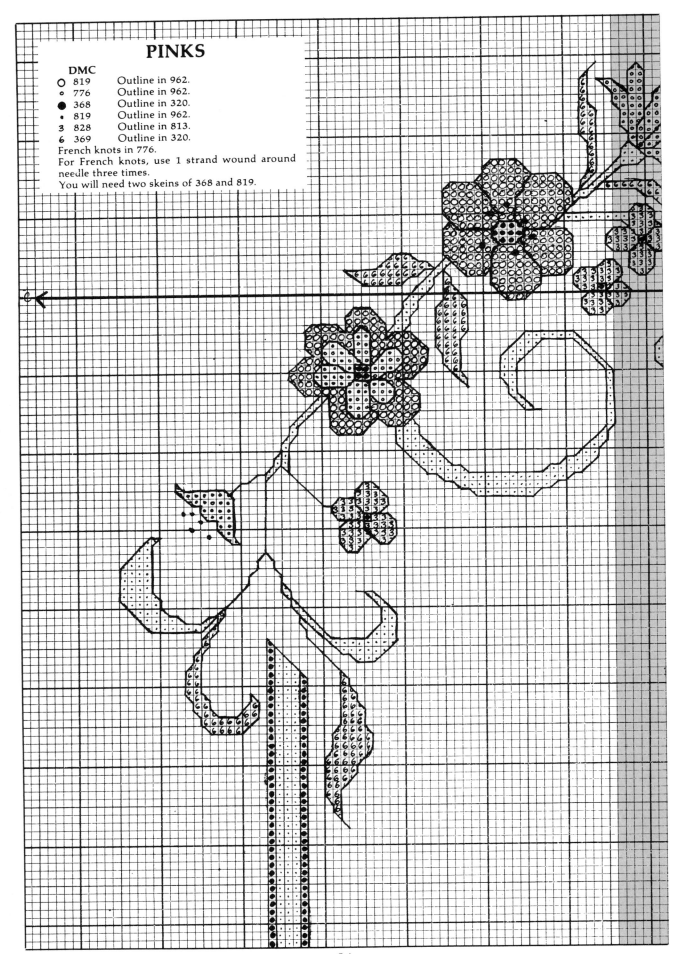

PINKS

DMC
○	819	Outline in 962.
∘	776	Outline in 962.
●	368	Outline in 320.
·	819	Outline in 962.
3	828	Outline in 813.
6	369	Outline in 320.

French knots in 776.
For French knots, use 1 strand wound around
needle three times.
You will need two skeins of 368 and 819.

MAUVES

DMC		
6	502	Outline in 501.
◦	224	Outline in 221.
○	223	Outline in 221.
●	221	Outline in 221.
3	225	Outline in 223.
·	504	Outline in 501.

French knots in 221.
For French knots, use 1 strand wound around needle three times.

SIMPLE ELEGANCE TABLECLOTH
(As pictured.)

	DMC	Bst
·	502	501
○	224	221
◦	223	221
●	221	221
3	225	223
6	504	501

(221) ribbon edge changed to 223.
(221) center on 225-3 flowers to 223.

BLUES & LAVENDERS

DMC

○	800	Outline in 792.
●	793	Outline in 792.
●	792	Outline in 792.
·	415	Outline in 414.
3	211	Outline in 208.
6	368	Outline in 320.

French knots in 792.
For French knots, use 1 strand wound around needle three times.
You will need two skeins of 792, 415, 800.

Shaded area indicates a portion of the chart from the previous page. Use as a guide in aligning stitches only.

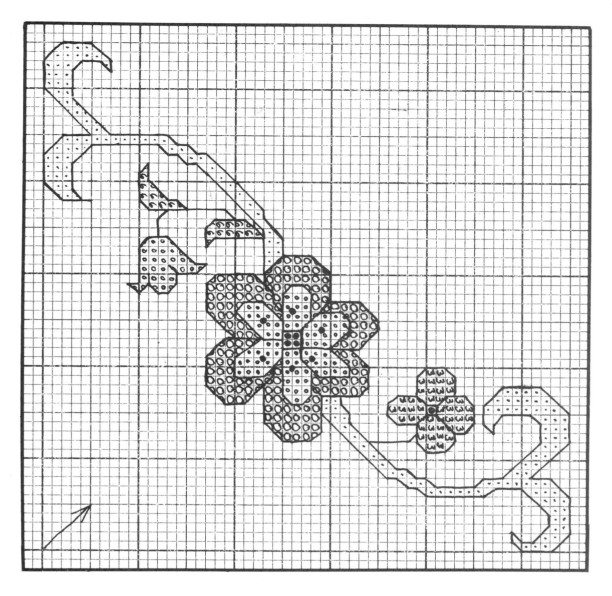

SIMPLE ELEGANCE
PLACEMATS

DMC
●	315	Outline in 315.
○	316	Outline in 315.
◐	778	Outline in 316.
3	932	Outline in 930.
6	503	Outline in 502.
•	841	Outline in 840.

French knots in 315.
For French knots, use 1 strand wound around needle three times.

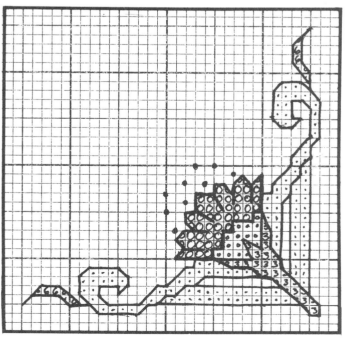

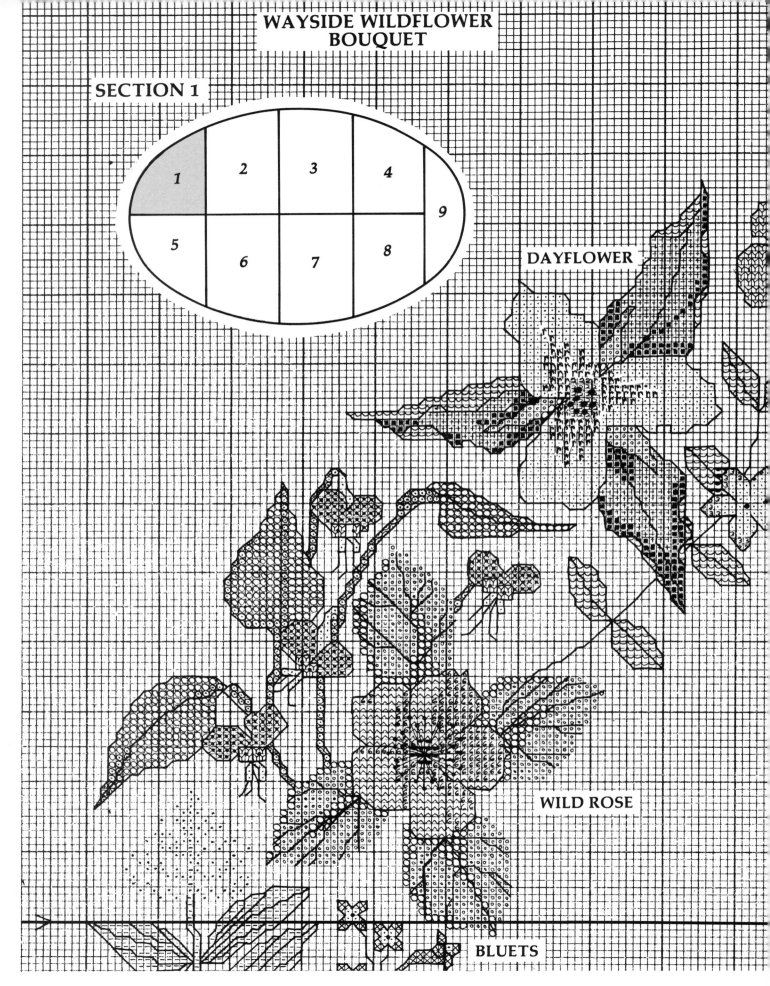

WAYSIDE WILDFLOWER
BOUQUET

SECTION 1

1 2 3 4
9
5 6 7 8

DAYFLOWER

WILD ROSE

BLUETS

98

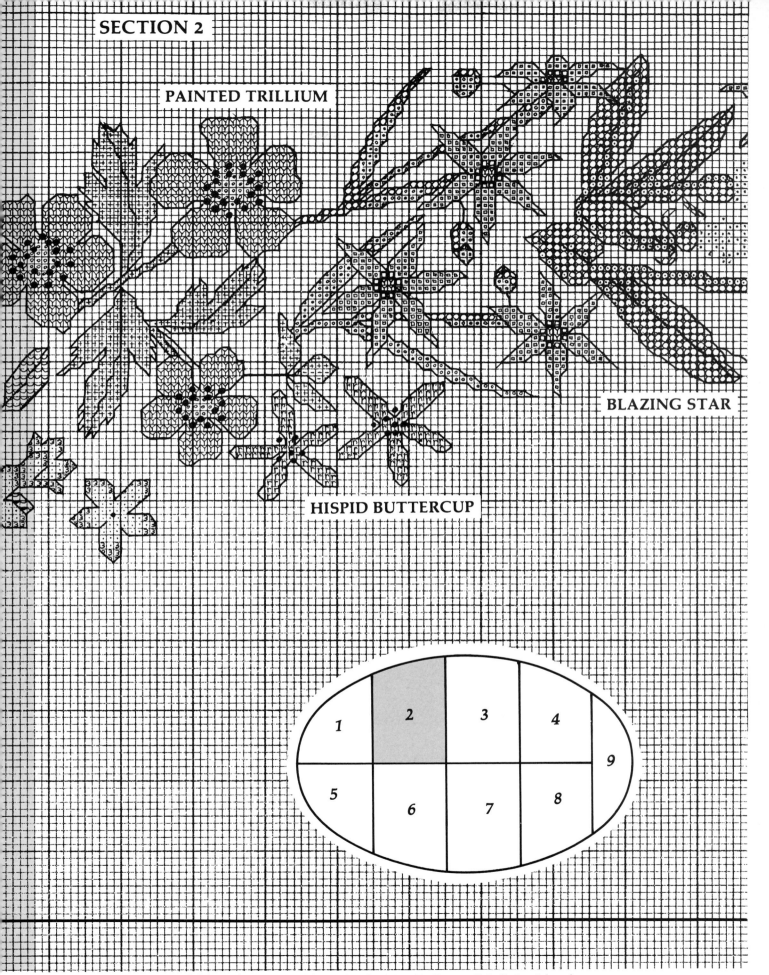

PAINTED TRILLIUM

BLAZING STAR

HISPID BUTTERCUP

Shaded area indicates a portion of the chart from the previous page. Use as a guide in aligning stitches only.

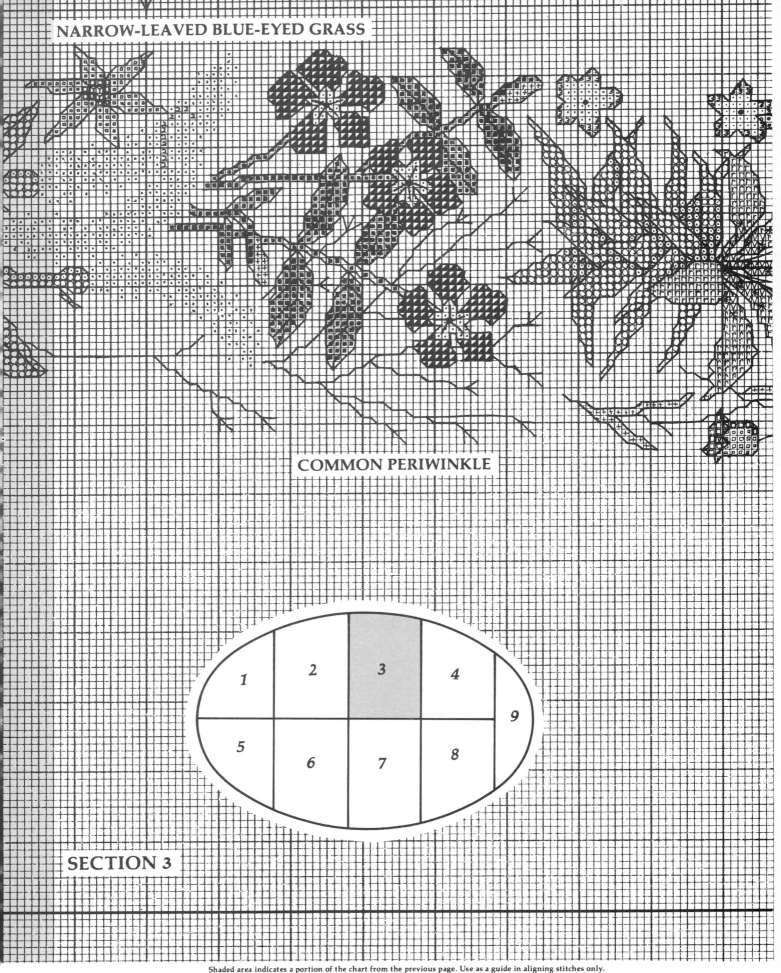

NARROW-LEAVED BLUE-EYED GRASS

COMMON PERIWINKLE

1	2	3	4
5	6	7	8

9

SECTION 3

Shaded area indicates a portion of the chart from the previous page. Use as a guide in aligning stitches only.

100

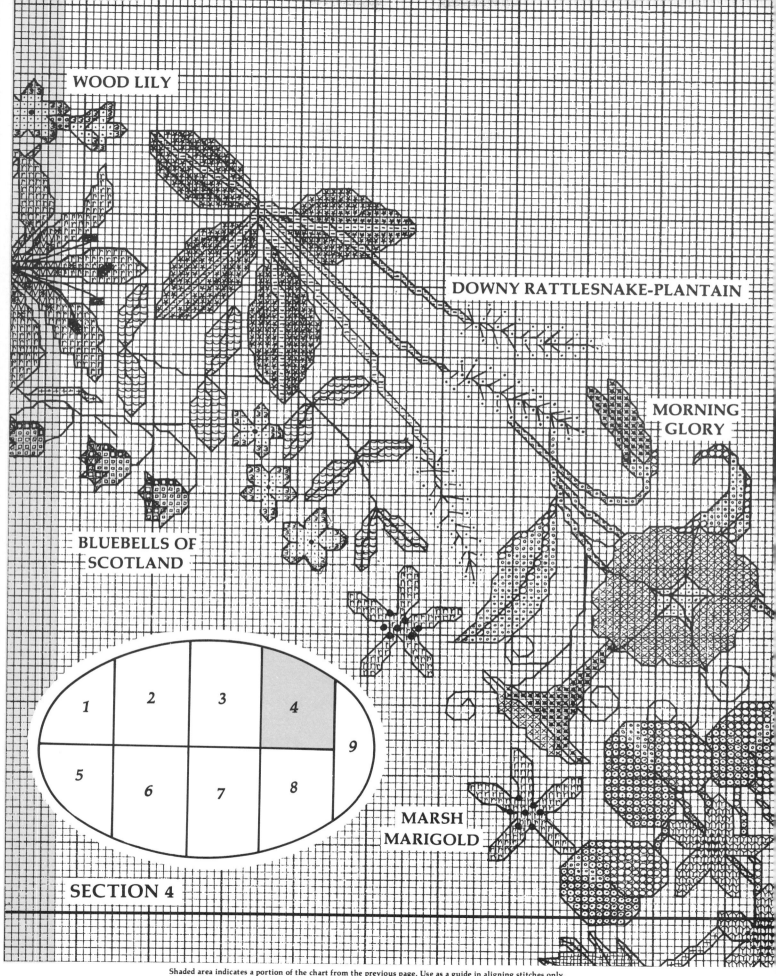

WOOD LILY

DOWNY RATTLESNAKE-PLANTAIN

MORNING
GLORY

BLUEBELLS OF
SCOTLAND

1	2	3	4	
5	6	7	8	9

SECTION 4

MARSH
MARIGOLD

Shaded area indicates a portion of the chart from the previous page. Use as a guide in aligning stitches only.

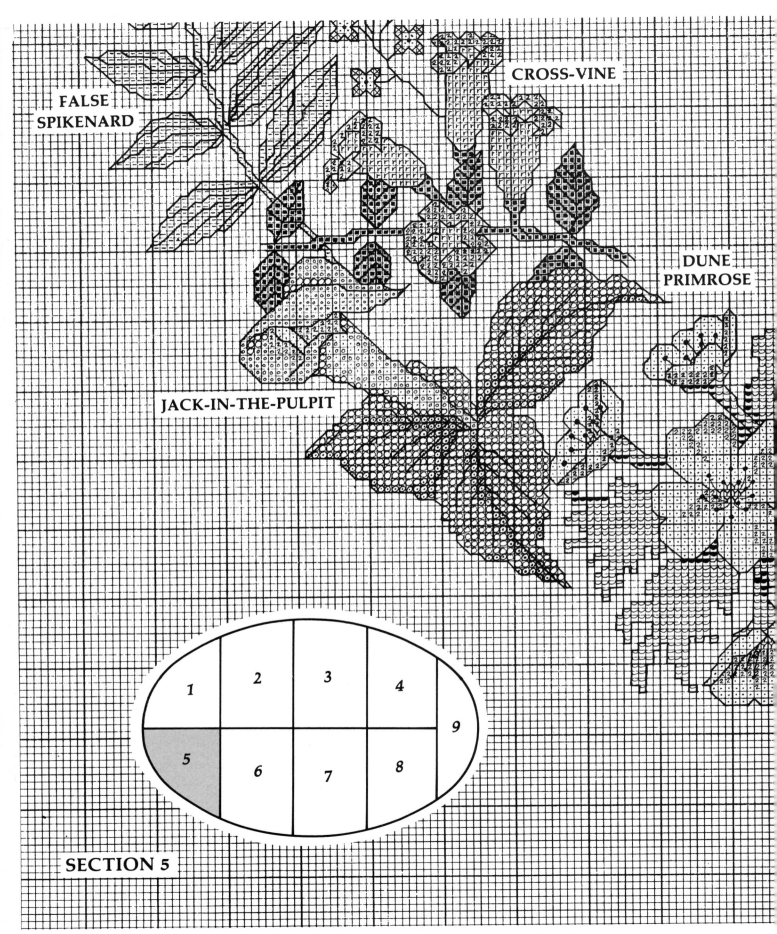

FALSE
SPIKENARD

CROSS-VINE

DUNE
PRIMROSE

JACK-IN-THE-PULPIT

1	2	3	4	
5	6	7	8	9

SECTION 5

Shaded area indicates a portion of the chart from the previous page. Use as a guide in aligning stitches only.

102

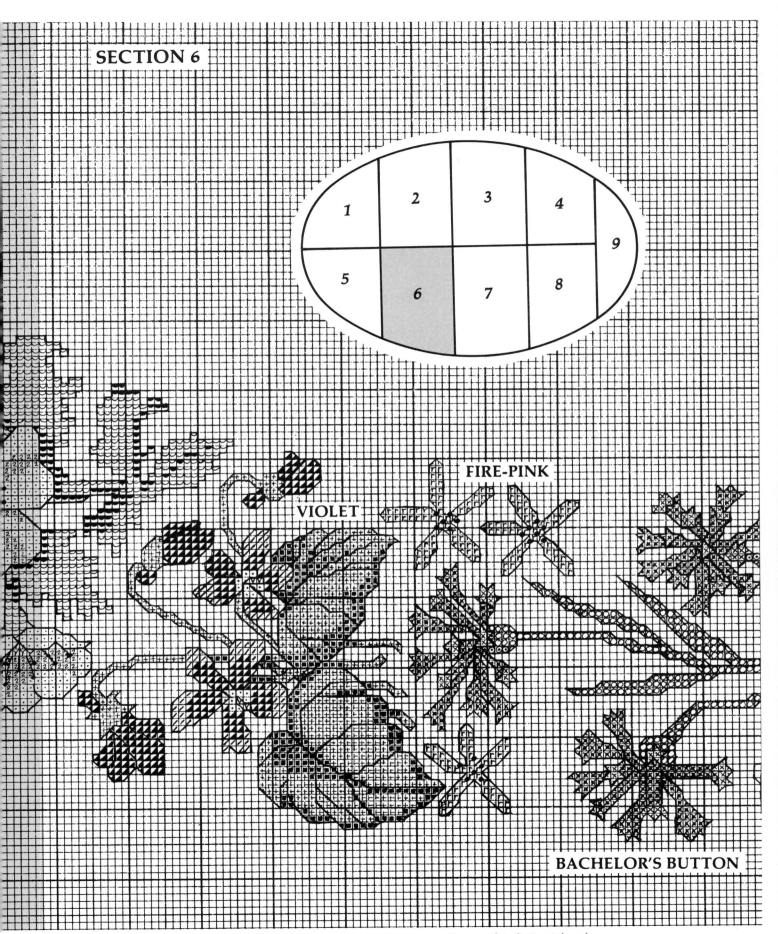

SECTION 6

1	2	3	4	
5	6	7	8	9

VIOLET

FIRE-PINK

BACHELOR'S BUTTON

Shaded area indicates a portion of the chart from the previous page. Use as a guide in aligning stitches only.

103

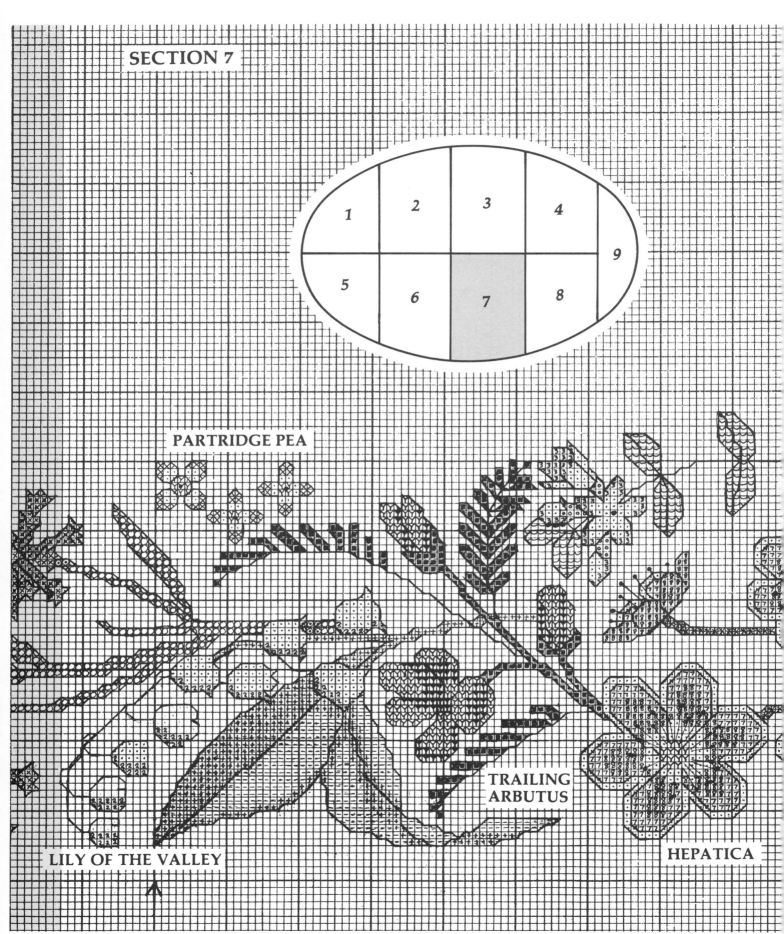

SECTION 7

| 1 | 2 | 3 | 4 | 9 |
| 5 | 6 | 7 | 8 | |

PARTRIDGE PEA

TRAILING ARBUTUS

LILY OF THE VALLEY

HEPATICA

Shaded area indicates a portion of the chart from the previous page. Use as a guide in aligning stitches only.

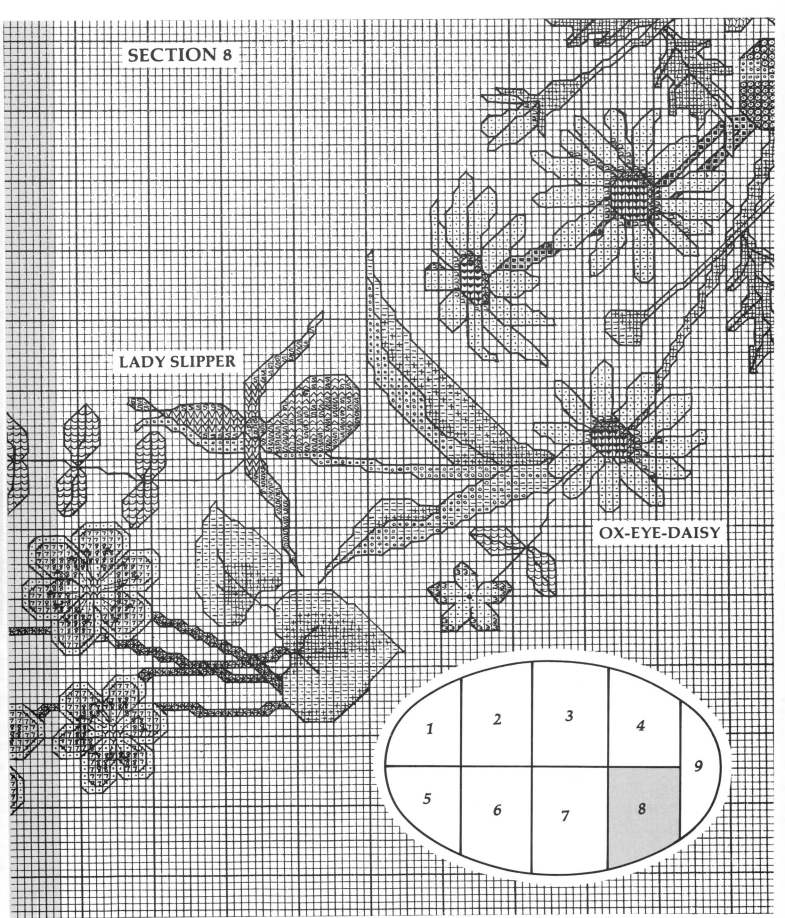

SECTION 8

LADY SLIPPER

OX-EYE-DAISY

1	2	3	4	9
5	6	7	8	

Shaded area indicates a portion of the chart from the previous page. Use as a guide in aligning stitches only.

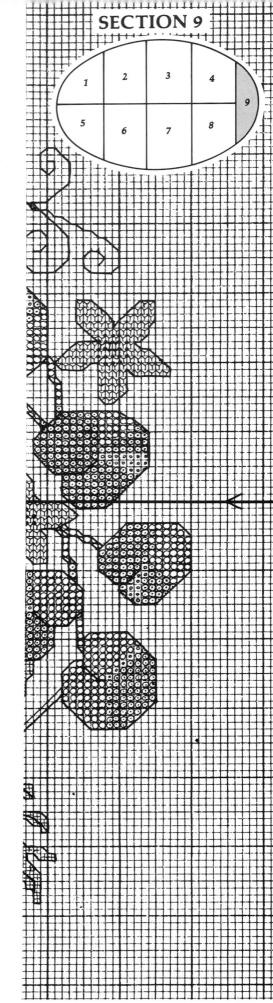

SECTION 9

1	2	3	4	9
5	6	7	8	

WAYSIDE WILDFLOWER BOUQUET

DMC Color

Symbol	Mauve fabric	Off-white grey or green fabric	Symbol	Mauve fabric	Off-white grey or green fabric
o	3053	472	3	225	3689
O	3052	581	∧	3326	957
⊙	3051	580	6	223	956
+	503	3364	S	3328	3328
+	502	3363	7	316	210
■	501	3362	8	315	208
◗	524	524	/	3042	350
◗	646	646	◢	327	333
Y	3047	744	□	341	341
T	3046	725	▢	793	793
V	758	721	x	813	794
ʌ	356	947	✗	312	798
✳	632	434	✶	502 & 3021	3363 & 535
•	Blanc Neige	Blanc Neige	*———	3371	3371
ı	Ecru	Ecru	*———	3021	535
r	3350	326			

*See Instructions.

Specific Instructions by Flower:

(Counter-clockwise beginning at left end of design. Colors given for mauve design, colors for off-white, grey or green design in parentheses.)

1. **False Spikenard** - outline and leaf veins 501 (3362).
2. **Bluets** - outline blooms 312 (798), stems 3051 (580), center French knots (medium-size) 356 (947).
3. **Cross-vine** - outline 3371 (3371).
4. **Jack-in-the-Pulpit** - outline 501 (3362).
5. **Dune Primrose** - outline 3371 (3371), medium French knots, connect to flower around yellow center with single strand running stitch 3047 (744).
6. **Violet** - outline stems & leaves 501 (3362), veins 3371 (3371), blooms 327 (333).
7. **Fire-pink** - (3 detached blooms) outline 3350 (326), large French knots 3047 (744).
8. **Bachelor's Button** - outline bloom 312 (798), outline leaves and stems 3051 (580).
9. **Lily of the Valley** - outline bells 3021 (535), stems, leaves and veins 3051 (580).
10. **Partridge Pea** - outline leaves and stems 501 (3362), blooms 3371 (3371).
11. **Trailing Arbutus** - center medium French knot 3046 (725), outline blooms 225 (3689), outline stems, veins, leaves 646 (646).
12. **Hepatica** - outline blooms 315 (208). Medium French knots connected to flower around yellow center with single strand running stitch (blanc neige). Stem 632, Outline leaves in 301.
13. **Lady Slipper** - outline flower 3328, veins in leaves 502.
14. **Ox-Eye-Daisy** - outline petals 3021 (535), outline centers 632 (434), outline stems, leaves and veins 501 (3362).
15. **Marsh Marigold** - outline petals 3046 (725), outline leaves and stems 501 (3362). Medium French knots 3046.
16. **Morning Glory** - outline petals and petal veins 312 (798). Do not outline between blue and white in center of flower. Outline leaves, stems and tendrils 3052 (581). Medium French knot 3047.
17. **Downy Rattlesnake-Plantain** - mix 1 strand each of 501 and 3021 (3363 and 535) for textured look to leaf. Leaf veins 503 (3364), outline leaves and stems 501 (3362).
18. **Bluebells of Scotland** - outline bells 312 (798), outline stems and leaves 501 (3362).
19. **Wood Lily** - fill in background. Connect stamens to center of flower with 2 strands running stitch 632 (434). Outline flowers 3350. Outline leaves 3051 (580).
20. **Common Periwinkle** - outline petals 327 (333). Do not outline between purple and white of flower centers. Over-stitch centers 327 (333). Outline stems and leaves 3051 (580), leaf veins 3053 (472). Medium French knots 3046.
21. **Blazing Star** - outline leaves and stems 501 (3362).
22. **Narrow-Leaved Blue-Eyed Grass** - outline blooms and tip of bud 793 (793), outline leaves and stems and unopened buds 502 (3363).
23. **Hispid Buttercup** - outline petals 3046 (725). Work large French knots 3046 (725). Outline stems, leaves and leaf veins 501 (3362).
24. **Painted Trillium** - work large French knots 3350 (326) over worked center. Outline leaves and veins 501 (3362). Outline flowers in 3371 (3371).
25. **Dayflower** - outline blue and white parts of flowers 312 (798). Medium French knots 632 (434) at centers of flowerettes. Outline stems, leaves and veins 3051 (580).
26. **Wild Rose** - work medium French knots 3046 (725), connect to center of rose with single strand 3047 (744) running stitch. Outline flower 3371 and leaf veins 502.

1. Cut 2½ yards of fabric.
2. Center the design.
3. Hem and attach lace.

Fabric: 2½ yards China Rose Oslo
Trim: 9 yards Devonshire Cream Victoria Lace

Stitched on 22-count over 2 threads.

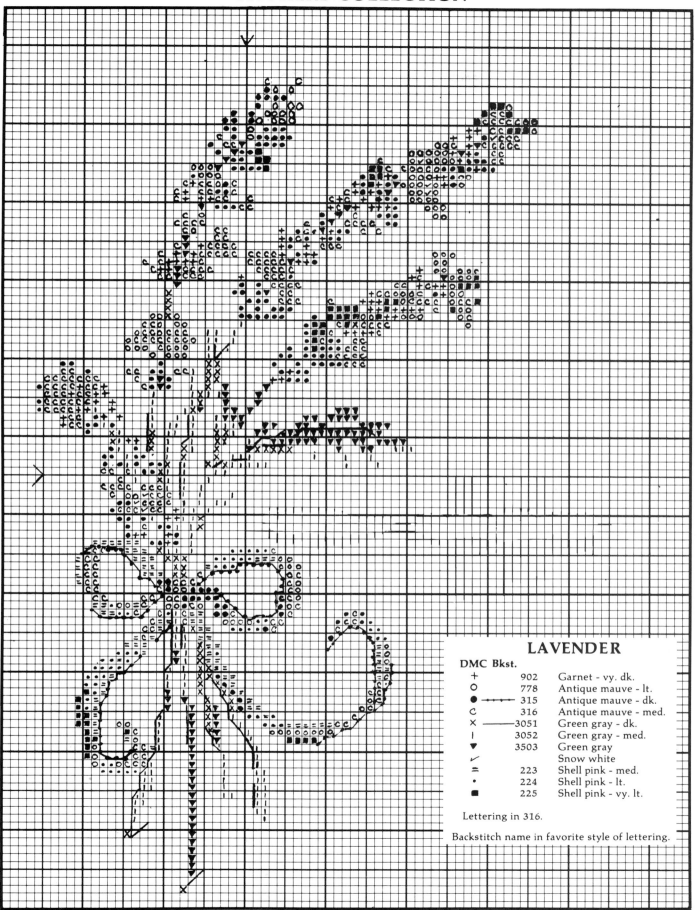

LAVENDER

DMC Bkst.

+	902	Garnet - vy. dk.
○	778	Antique mauve - lt.
●	315	Antique mauve - dk.
C	316	Antique mauve - med.
×	3051	Green gray - dk.
I	3052	Green gray - med.
▼	3503	Green gray
✓		Snow white
=	223	Shell pink - med.
•	224	Shell pink - lt.
■	225	Shell pink - vy. lt.

Lettering in 316.

Backstitch name in favorite style of lettering.

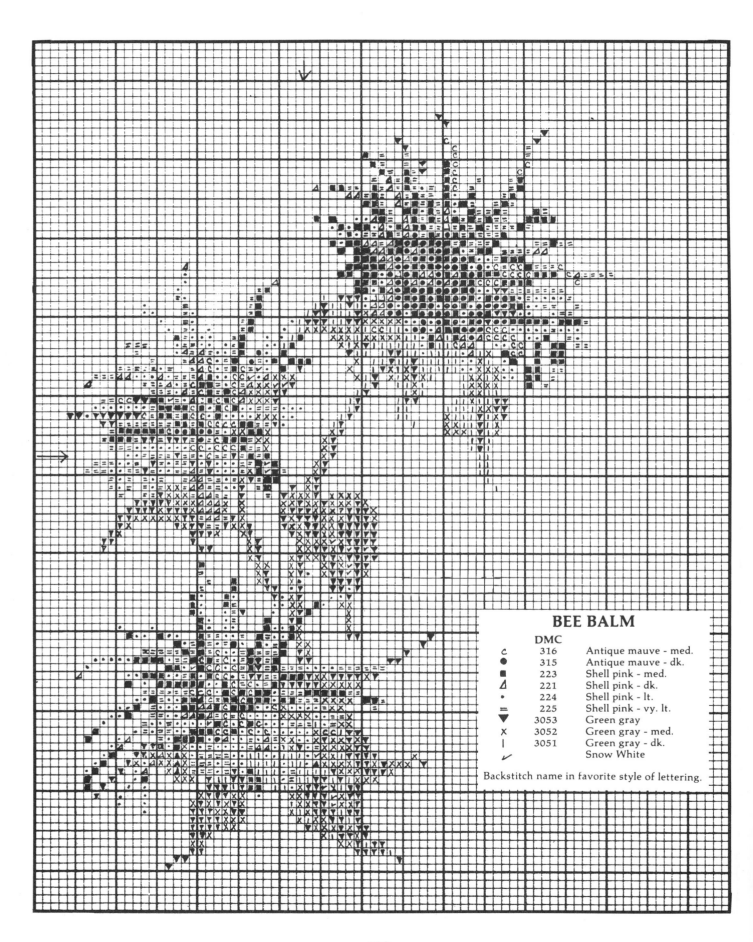

BEE BALM

	DMC	
c	316	Antique mauve - med.
●	315	Antique mauve - dk.
▣	223	Shell pink - med.
◮	221	Shell pink - dk.
•	224	Shell pink - lt.
=	225	Shell pink - vy. lt.
▼	3053	Green gray
X	3052	Green gray - med.
I	3051	Green gray - dk.
✓		Snow White

Backstitch name in favorite style of lettering.

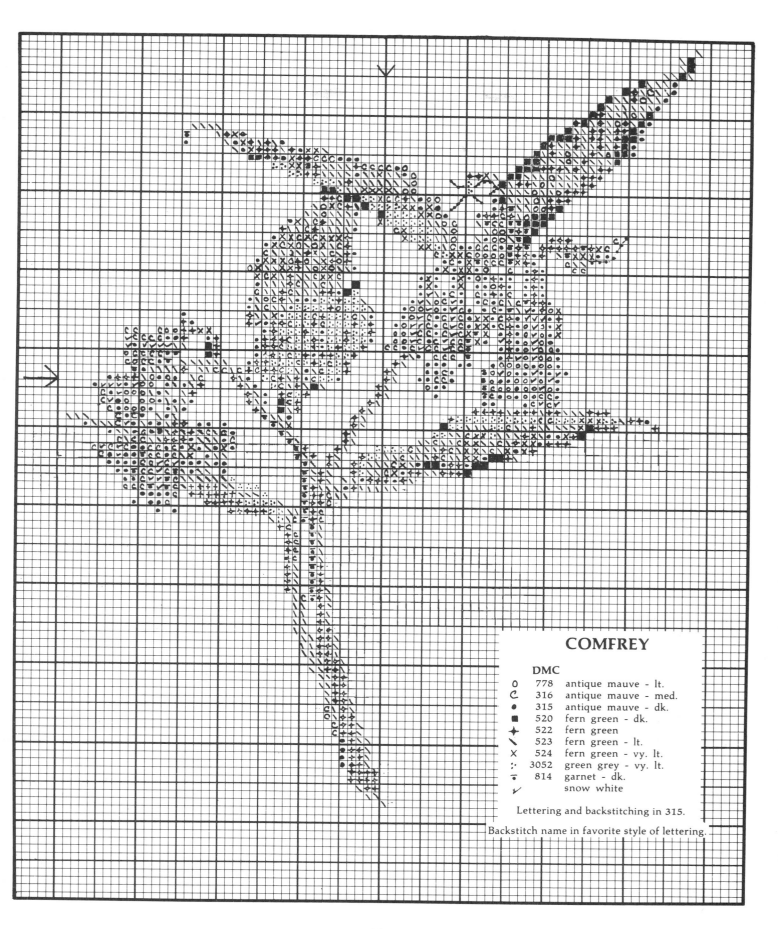

COMFREY

DMC

O	778	antique mauve - lt.
C	316	antique mauve - med.
●	315	antique mauve - dk.
■	520	fern green - dk.
✦	522	fern green
\	523	fern green - lt.
X	524	fern green - vy. lt.
∴	3052	green grey - vy. lt.
⊤	814	garnet - dk.
↙		snow white

Lettering and backstitching in 315.

Backstitch name in favorite style of lettering.

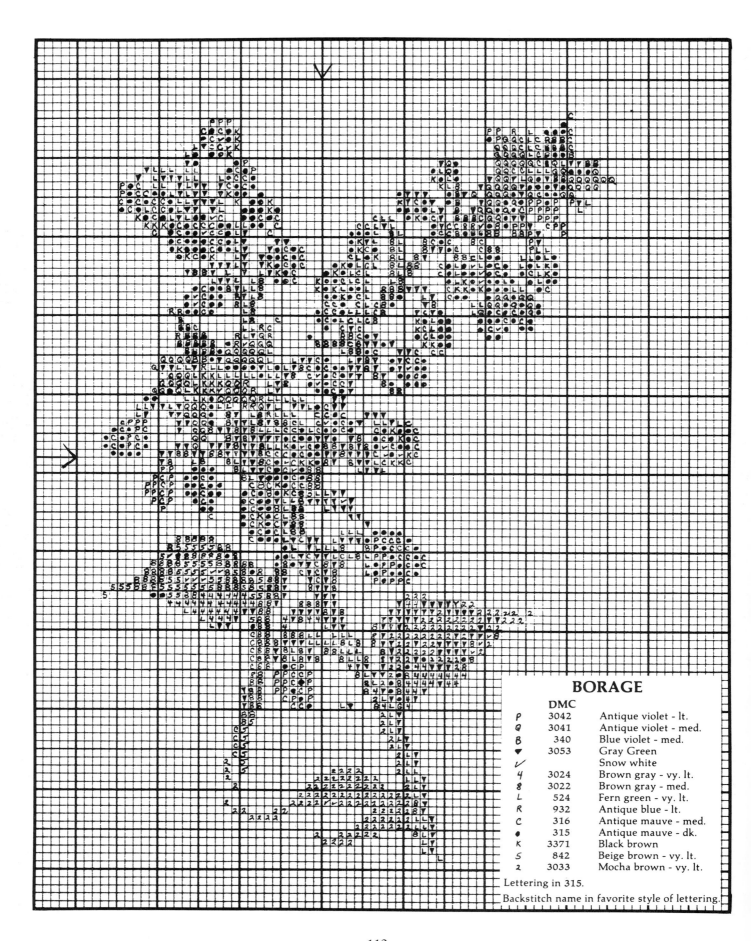

BORAGE

	DMC	
P	3042	Antique violet - lt.
Q	3041	Antique violet - med.
B	340	Blue violet - med.
▼	3053	Gray Green
∨		Snow white
4	3024	Brown gray - vy. lt.
8	3022	Brown gray - med.
L	524	Fern green - vy. lt.
R	932	Antique blue - lt.
C	316	Antique mauve - med.
●	315	Antique mauve - dk.
K	3371	Black brown
S	842	Beige brown - vy. lt.
2	3033	Mocha brown - vy. lt.

Lettering in 315.

Backstitch name in favorite style of lettering.

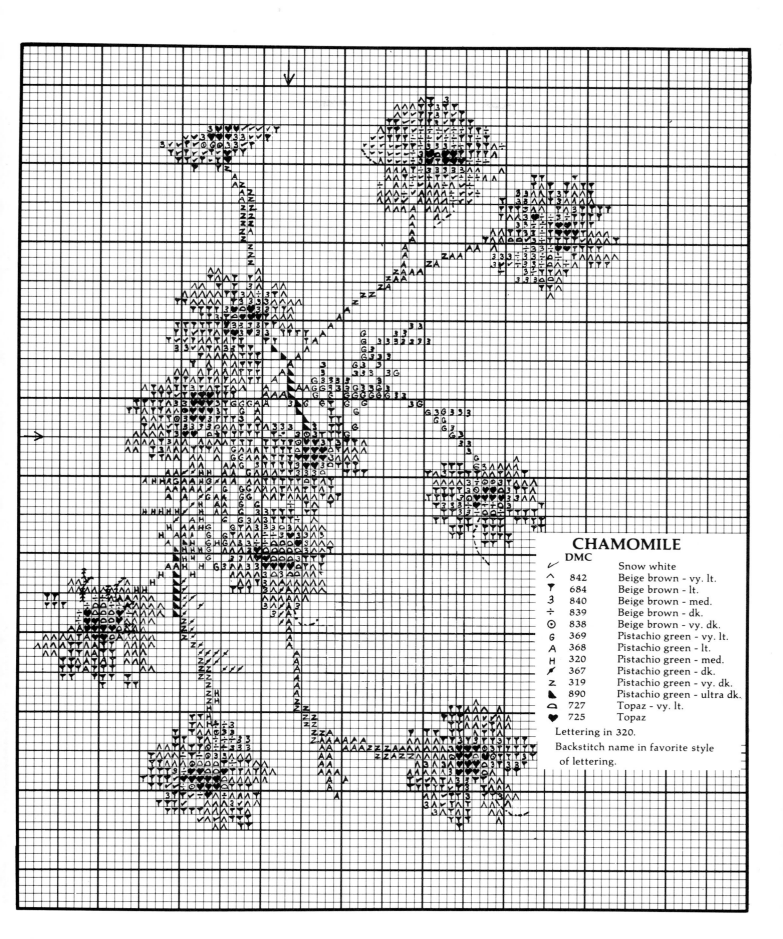

CHAMOMILE

DMC

✓		Snow white
∧	842	Beige brown - vy. lt.
Y	684	Beige brown - lt.
3	840	Beige brown - med.
÷	839	Beige brown - dk.
⊙	838	Beige brown - vy. dk.
G	369	Pistachio green - vy. lt.
A	368	Pistachio green - lt.
H	320	Pistachio green - med.
∕	367	Pistachio green - dk.
Z	319	Pistachio green - vy. dk.
◣	890	Pistachio green - ultra dk.
◿	727	Topaz - vy. lt.
♥	725	Topaz

Lettering in 320.

Backstitch name in favorite style
of lettering.

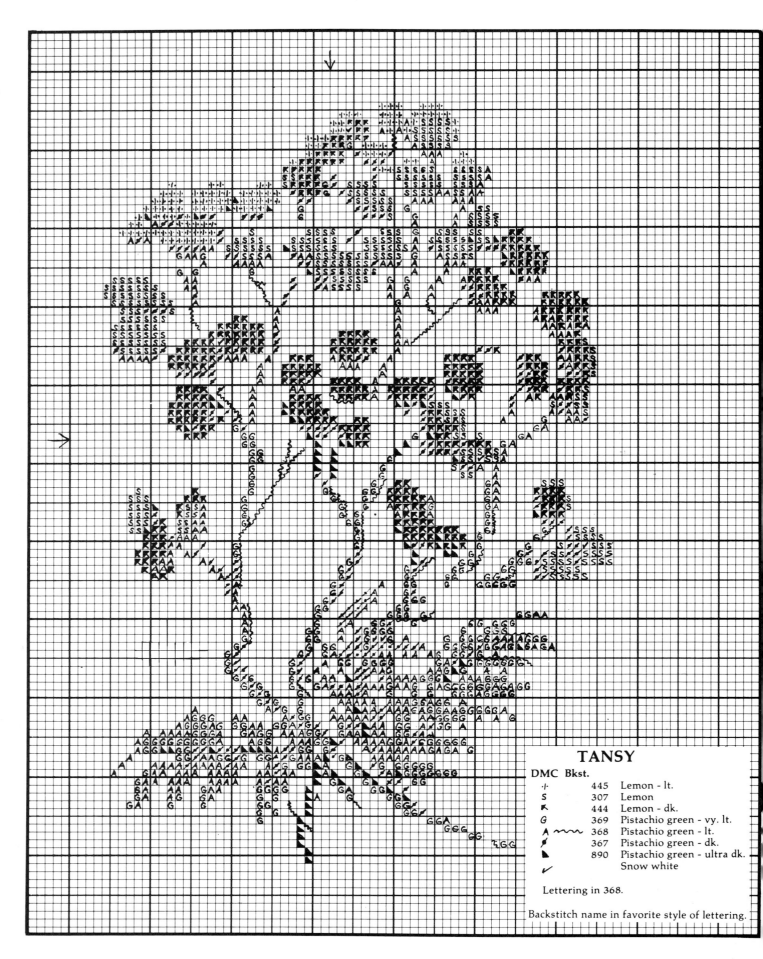

TANSY

DMC Bkst.

·/·	445	Lemon - lt.
S	307	Lemon
K	444	Lemon - dk.
G	369	Pistachio green - vy. lt.
A ~~~	368	Pistachio green - lt.
◢	367	Pistachio green - dk.
◣	890	Pistachio green - ultra dk.
✔		Snow white

Lettering in 368.

Backstitch name in favorite style of lettering.